"After sampling dozens of Lindy's creations, I can tell you that without exception, I enjoyed each one! While I don't have a restricted diet, I turn to Lindy's recipes often and hope to be among the first to get her new book! I love to entertain and with Lindy's uncomplicated, delicious recipes, I get compliments from all of my friends with or without restricted diets."
~Judy Thiel Price, Project Management Coordinator, NWTC

"Mrs. Lindy's gluten free desserts are amazing! Each recipe is flavorful and tastes awesome."
~Rohan Gala, age 16

Published by Tintrí Press

Copyright © 2020 Lindy Stein
Photos © 2020 Lindy Stein
Cover Design © 2020 Kristen Joy Laidig
Interior Artwork © 2020 Kristen Joy Laidig

Follow Lindy on Facebook at:
Facebook.com/LindysGlutenFreeGoodies

Learn more about Lindy's businesses at:
LindysLessons.com

All rights reserved. No part of this publication may be reproduced or transmitted in any form or by any means, including informational storage and retrieval systems, without permission in writing from the copyright holder, except for brief quotations in a review.

This book's content is for informational purposes only and is not intended to replace professional nutritional advice.

ISBN 13: 978-0-9852577-0-5

First Tintrí Press printing, January 2020
Printed in the United States of America

Introduction

The flour I use exclusively is Bob's Red Mill Gluten-Free All-Purpose Baking Flour. It is a bean based flour (garbanzo bean, fava bean, sorghum flour, tapioca flour and potato flour), thus very bitter. I advise you if you are a "batter eating" type of baker – DO NOT DO THAT…..with this flour anyway! I do not know what happens in the baking process, but by some magic, that bitterness goes away and these goodies are sooooo amazingly tasty! With this all-purpose flour mix, you will need a binder. All my recipes use xanthan gum. It is a powder that you mix into the dry ingredients and the amount will vary depending on the type of baking you are doing – cookies use ¼ teaspoon per 1 cup flour, cakes and brownies: ½ teaspoon per 1 cup flour and sweet breads and muffins: ¾ teaspoon per 1 cup flour. Do not add it to the wet ingredients as it will not work as effectively.

One more note – Bob's Red Mill Gluten-Free All-Purpose Baking Flour can be substituted for any recipe that calls for regular (wheat based) all-purpose flour on a one-to-one basis. (For example, if the recipe you want to convert calls for 1 ½ cups regular all-purpose flour, you will use 1 ½ cups GF all-purpose flour.)

I buy my flour in bulk (25 pound bag) from a small country store as well as the xanthan gum. Both the flour and xanthan gum can be purchased in almost all grocery stores that sell gluten free products, ie – Walmart, Meijer, Festival, Kroger, etc.

Bob's Red Mill also makes another gluten-free all-purpose flour called "Gluten-Free 1 to 1 Baking Flour". It is a rice flour base: Sweet White Rice Flour, Whole Grain Brown Rice Flour, Potato Starch, Whole Grain Sweet White Sorghum Flour, Tapioca Flour, Xanthan Gum and as you can see, the xanthan gum is already in the mix. I have not tried this mix as I am totally pleased with the results of the bean flour mix and am not a fan of rice flour based treats. Everyone's palate is different so please experiment and find out what works best for you and your family.

Happy baking!

Lindy Stein

"Lindy is a multi-talented, highly energetic, musically gifted person as well as being super talented in the cooking arena. In the years I've known her, the many mouth-watering treats she has bestowed upon myself and fellow martial artists often lead us to sparring competitions for whom the victor goes the sweet spoils."

~Sensei Herb Blue, Co-Owner and Head Instructor: Total Self Defense, LLC

Table of Contents

Introduction 3
Table of Contents 4

Bars & Brownies 7
Black Bottom Banana Bars 10
Brownie Pizza 11
Caramel Pecan Fudge Brownies 12
Chocolate Peanut Butter Brownies 13
Pecan Brownie Shortbread Bars 14
Chocolate Raspberry Truffle Brownies 15
Deadly Fudge Brownies 16
Everything But the Kitchen Sink Brownies 17
Fudgy Oat Bars 18
Peanut Butter Chip Bars 19
Polka Dotted Brownies 20
Raspberry Chocolate Bars 21
Todd's Brownies 22
Wonder Bars 23
Frosted Zucchini Brownies 24

Breads & Muffins 25
Apple Nut Muffins 28
Carol's Spicy Zucchini Bread 29
Chocolate Chip Zucchini Muffins 30
Double Chocolate Pumpkin Bread 31
Give Thanks Muffins 32
Cinnamon Raisin Bread 33
Lemon Blueberry Biscuits 34
Peanut Streusel Bread 35
Pumpkin Apple Muffins 36
Strawberry Bread with Berry Spread 37
New Blueberry Muffins 38
Ping's Pumpkin Bread 39
Lemon Zucchini Bread 40
Ginger Cranberry Muffins 41
Dutch Apple Bread 42

Cakes & Cupcakes 43
Almost Totally Free Chocolate Cupcakes 46

Chocolate Cream Cheese Cupcakes 47
Beverly's Lemon Pound Cake 48
Banana Cupcakes. 49
Chocolate Sour Cream Cake 50
Old Fashioned Crumb Cake 51
Chocolate Peanut Surprise Cupcakes. 52
Spiced Zucchini Cupcakes with Caramel Frosting. 53
Cream Filled Carrot Cake 54
Red Velvet Cupcakes 55
Pineapple Cake with Coconut-Pecan Frosting. 56
Cinnamon-Caramel Cupcakes. 57
Mexican Cake. 58
Apple Cake with Caramel Sauce. 59
Texas Sheet Cake. 60

Pies & Cheesecakes 61
Blueberry Cheesecake Pie 64
Applesauce Walnut Pie 65
Brownie Bottom Fudge Caramel Cheesecake. 66
Caramel Apple Pie with Pecans 67
Chocolate Chip Cookie Dough Cheesecake. 68
Mystery Pecan Pie 69
Rhubarb-Strawberry Pie 70
Chocolate Chip Pie 72
S'mores Cheesecake 73
Strawberry Pie 74
Coconut Cream Pie. 75
Turtle Pumpkin Cheesecake 76
Mock Apple Pie. 78
Tin Roof Fudge Pie. 79

Cookies 81
Vintage Sugar Cookies. 84
S'mores Sandwich Cookies. 85
Classic Oatmeal Raisin Cookies 86
Reverse S'oreos. 87
Triple Chip Peanut Butter Cookies. 88
Frosted Pumpkin Cookies 89
Chocolate Filled Snowballs 90
Cranberry Chip Cookies. 91
Snickerdoodles 92
Double Chocolate Dream Cookies 93
Cherry Chocolate Shortbread Cookies 94
Spritz. 95
Gingerbread Cut-Out Cookies. 96

  Chocolate Raspberry Cookies 97
  Breakfast Cookies 98
  Peanut Butter Sandwich Cookies 99
  Classic Chocolate Chip Cookies 100

Other Desserts 101

  Applesauce Drop Donuts 104
  Blueberry Torte 105
  Butter Brickle Biscotti 106
  Mini Peanut Butter Cup Cheesecakes 107
  Caramel Apple Crisp 108
  Pumpkin Whoopie Pies 109
  Strawberry Oat-Fashioned Dessert 110
  Brownie Whoops 111
  Blackberry Cobbler 112
  Pumpkin Roll 113
  Blueberry Apple Crisp 114
  Brownie Trifle 115
  Perfect Hot Fudge Sauce 116

Breakfast 117

  Pumpkin Waffles 120
  Banana Blueberry Pancakes 121
  Berries 'n Cream French Toast 122
  Blueberry Poppy Seed Brunch Cake 123
  "LaValliere" Breakfast Puffs 124
  Caramel French Toast 125
  Crispy Granola Bars 126
  Nutty French Toast 127
  Bonnie's Excellent Granola 128

Order Books 129

Bars & Brownies

"When it comes to chocolate, resistance is futile."

-Regina Brett

Don't you just hate it when a treat looks really chocolatey (that is if you like chocolate), and you bite into said treat and it really lacks that 'wow' factor that you were anticipating? One of the 'secrets' I have stumbled upon is to add considerably more cocoa or whatever type of chocolate the recipe calls for to give the brownies, cookies or cake that extra 'wow' factor. For your information, all of the recipes in this section do have some sort of chocolate in them.

Get ready to "WOW" your tastebuds with these recipes!

Black Bottom Banana Bars
Brownie Pizza
Caramel Pecan Fudge Brownies
Chocolate Peanut Butter Brownies
Pecan Brownie Shortbread Bars
Chocolate Raspberry Truffle Brownies
Deadly Fudge Brownies
Everything But The Kitchen Sink Brownies
Fudgy Oat Bars
Peanut Butter Chip Bars
Polka Dotted Brownies
Raspberry Chocolate Bars
Todd's Brownies
Wonder Bars
Frosted Zucchini Brownies

Black Bottom Banana Bars

½ cup (1 stick) butter, softened
1 cup granulated sugar
1 egg
1 teaspoon vanilla extract
1 ½ cups mashed ripe bananas (about 3 medium)
1 ½ cups GF all-purpose baking flour
1 teaspoon baking powder
1 teaspoon baking soda
⅝ teaspoon xanthan gum
½ teaspoon salt
½ cup baking cocoa

Preheat oven to 350°. Grease or foil line and grease a 13-in. x 9-in. x 2-in. baking pan.

In a large mixing bowl, cream together butter and sugar until light and fluffy. Beat in egg and vanilla. Stir in the bananas.

In another bowl, whisk together flour and next four ingredients. Gradually add to butter mixture.

Divide batter in half. Add cocoa to one half of batter and spread in prepared pan. Carefully spread remaining batter on top and swirl together with a knife.

Bake for 20-25 minutes or until a toothpick inserted near the center comes out clean.

Cool on wire rack.

Yield: 2 ½ - 3 dozen

"Life is full of banana skins. You slip, you carry on."
—Daphne Guinness

Brownie Pizza

BROWNIE:
¾ cup GF all-purpose baking flour
⅜ teaspoon xanthan gum
½ cup (1 stick) butter, cubed
2 ounces unsweetened baking chocolate
1 ounce semi-sweet baking chocolate
1 cup granulated sugar
2 eggs, lightly beaten

FROSTING:
1 cup powdered sugar
⅓ cup creamy peanut butter
1 ½ teaspoons vanilla extract
2 to 4 tablespoons milk

TOPPINGS:
¾ cup plain M&M's (more or less to taste)
½ cup flaked coconut
½ cup chopped peanuts
½ cup semisweet chocolate chips

Preheat oven to 350°. Grease a 12-in. pizza pan.

In a small bowl, whisk together the flour and xanthan gum.

In a small saucepan over low heat, melt the butter, chocolate and sugar. Cook and stir until well combined.

Remove from heat and stir in flour mixture until smooth. Add eggs and beat until smooth.

Spread onto prepared pan and bake for 15 minutes or until a toothpick inserted near the center comes out clean. Cool completely.

For frosting, in a small bowl, beat sugar and next three ingredients until desired spreading consistency is achieved.

Spread over brownie crust. Sprinkle with topping ingredients.

Yield: 8-10 servings.

Caramel Pecan Fudge Brownies

¾ cup (1 ½ sticks) butter
4 ounces unsweetened baking chocolate
4 eggs
2 cups granulated sugar
1 ¼ cups GF all-purpose baking flour
½ teaspoon xanthan gum
2 teaspoons vanilla extract
1 cup chopped pecans
1 package (12 ounces) semi-sweet chocolate chips, *divided*
1 package (11-14 ounces) caramels*
¼ cup heavy cream

Preheat oven to 350°. Line a 13-in. x 9-in. x 2-in. baking pan with foil. Generously grease foil.

Melt butter and chocolate in the top of a double boiler, stirring often until smooth. Transfer to a large bowl.

Whisk in eggs and next four ingredients. Stir in pecans.

Spread half the batter into prepared pan. Sprinkle with 1 cup chocolate chips.

In medium saucepan, melt caramels and cream over medium-low heat until smooth. Pour this mixture evenly over batter in pan. Carefully spread with remaining batter – use small spoonfuls to ease in spreading out batter. Sprinkle with remaining 1 cup chocolate chips. Batter will spread out as it bakes.

Bake for 35-40 minutes or until top is dry to the touch. Let cool completely in pan on wire rack.

Lift foil from pan and cut into squares.**

Yield: 24 brownies

*Recipe was tested using Kraft Caramel Bits

**Heat large knife up under hot water to ease in cutting. Clean knife after each cut with hot water.

> "Caramel gives chocolate a run for its money."
> —Sherry Yard

Chocolate Peanut Butter Brownies

BROWNIE:
3 eggs
1 cup (2 sticks) butter, melted
2 teaspoons vanilla extract
2 cups granulated sugar
1 ¼ cups GF all-purpose baking flour
¾ cup baking cocoa
½ teaspoon xanthan gum
½ teaspoon baking powder
¼ teaspoon salt
1 cup milk chocolate chips

FILLING:
2 packages (8 ounces each) cream cheese*, softened
¾ cup creamy peanut butter
¼ cup granulated sugar
1 egg
1 tablespoon milk

*Recipe was tested using one package 1/3 less fat cream cheese and one package regular cream cheese.

Preheat oven to 350°. Grease or foil line and grease a 13-in. x 9-in. x 2-in. baking pan.

In a large mixing bowl, beat the eggs, butter and vanilla until smooth.

In a medium bowl, whisk together the sugar and next five ingredients. Gradually add to egg mixture. Stir in chocolate chips. Set aside 1 cup for topping. Spread remaining batter into prepared baking pan.

In a small mixing bowl, beat the cream cheese, peanut butter and sugar until smooth. Beat in egg and milk on low until just moistened. Carefully spread over batter.

Drop reserved batter by tablespoonfuls over filling. Using a knife, swirl topping through the cream cheese layer.

Bake for 45-50 minutes or until a toothpick inserted in the center comes out clean.

Do not overbake. Cool on a wire rack.

Pecan Brownie Shortbread Bars

CRUST:
1 cup (2 sticks) butter, softened
½ cup powdered sugar
2 cups GF all-purpose baking flour
½ teaspoon xanthan gum
¼ teaspoon ground cinnamon
¼ teaspoon salt

BROWNIE:
3 ounces semi-sweet baking chocolate
3 ounces bittersweet baking chocolate
½ cup (1 stick) butter, softened
1 cup brown sugar, firmly packed
2 eggs
¼ cup GF all-purpose baking flour
1 ½ teaspoons vanilla extract
¼ teaspoon salt
2 cups pecan halves

CRUST:

Preheat oven to 350°. Line a 13"x9" baking pan with foil and coat with butter.

In a medium mixing bowl, beat together butter and powdered sugar until well combined.

In a separate bowl, whisk together the flour and next three ingredients; gradually add to butter mixture until well combined.

Spoon dough into prepared baking dish and press dough into an even layer. This will be tricky as the dough is quite sticky. (I kept a stick of butter nearby and continued to coat my fingers with it to keep the dough from sticking to my fingers.)

Bake for 20 minutes or until lightly golden brown.

BROWNIE:

While crust is baking, melt chocolate in a double boiler, stir until smooth. Remove from heat.

In medium mixing bowl, cream the butter and brown sugar until light and fluffy. Add the eggs, one at a time, beating well after each addition.

Add flour, vanilla and salt. Beat until well combined.

Add melted chocolate, mix well.

Carefully spread the brownie batter over the shortbread crust.

Press the pecan halves into the batter.

Bake for 30 minutes or until top is set. Do not overbake–you want the brownie layer to be chewy.

Cool completely before cutting into bars.

Store in airtight container.

Chocolate Raspberry Truffle Brownies

BROWNIE:

½ cup (1 stick) butter, cubed

¾ cup semi-sweet chocolate chips

½ cup 60% bittersweet chocolate chips

2 eggs

¾ cup packed brown sugar

1 teaspoon hot chocolate mix*

2 tablespoons water

¾ cup GF all-purpose baking flour

½ teaspoon baking powder

3/8 teaspoon xanthan gum

FILLING:

½ cup semi-sweet chocolate chips

½ cup 60% bittersweet chocolate chips

1 package (8 ounces) cream cheese, softened**

¼ cup powdered sugar

1/3 cup seedless red raspberry jam

GLAZE:

¼ cup semi-sweet chocolate chips***

1 teaspoon shortening

*Instant coffee granules may be substituted

**Recipe was tested using 1/3 less fat cream cheese

***Raspberry chocolate chips are a great substitution, if available, for the glaze

Preheat oven to 350°. Foil line a 9-in. square baking pan. Grease foil.

In a microwave safe bowl (or in a double boiler on the stove) melt butter and chocolate chips; stir until smooth.

In a large mixing bowl, beat eggs and brown sugar until blended. Dissolve hot chocolate mix in water; add to egg mixture. Beat in chocolate until well blended.

In a medium bowl, whisk together the flour and next two ingredients. Gradually add to chocolate mixture, stirring until just combined.

Spread in prepared baking pan and bake for 30-35 minutes or until a toothpick inserted near center comes out clean. Cool on wire rack.

For filling, in a microwave safe bowl (or in a double boiler on the stove) melt chocolate chips; stir until smooth. Cool.

In a small bowl, beat cream cheese and powdered sugar until smooth. Beat in jam. Stir in melted chocolate; spread over cooled brownies.

For glaze, in a microwave safe bowl (or in a double boiler on the stove) melt chocolate chips and shortening; stir until smooth. Drizzle over filling. Chill before cutting. Store leftovers in refrigerator.

Note: To cut brownies – lift foil liner out of pan, warm a large knife with hot water and slice through brownie. Rinse knife off with hot water after each cut.

Deadly Fudge Brownies

4 ounces unsweetened baking chocolate
1 cup (2 sticks) butter, no substitutes
4 eggs
2 cups granulated sugar
1 teaspoon vanilla extract
1 cup GF all-purpose baking flour
½ teaspoon xanthan gum
1 cup (6 ounces) semi-sweet chocolate chips
1 cup chopped nuts, optional

Preheat oven to 350°. Grease or foil line and grease a 13-in. x 9-in. x 2-in. baking pan.

In a microwave safe bowl, melt baking chocolate and butter in 30 second intervals; stirring until smooth and completely melted. Chocolate and butter may also be melted using a double boiler on stove top.

In a medium mixing bowl, beat eggs, sugar and vanilla for 1-2 minutes or until light and lemon-colored. Beat in chocolate mixture.

In a separate bowl, whisk together the flour and xanthan gum. Add flour to chocolate mixture; stir just until combined. Fold in chocolate chips and nuts if desired.

Spoon into prepared baking dish and bake for 25-30 minutes or until a toothpick inserted near the center comes out with moist crumbs.

Cool on wire rack.

Yield: 16-20 servings

"After a salty meal, you need a little bit of sweet. This is living, not cheating."
-Ali Landry

Everything But the Kitchen Sink Brownies

1 cup GF all-purpose baking flour

½ cup (rounded) unsweetened baking cocoa

1 teaspoon baking powder

½ teaspoon (rounded) ground cinnamon

½ teaspoon salt

½ teaspoon xanthan gum

½ cup (1 stick) butter

1 cup packed brown sugar

1 large egg

2 teaspoons vanilla extract

½ cup toffee pieces

¾ cup flaked coconut, *divided*

¾ chopped pecans, *divided*

1 cup semi-sweet chocolate chips

Preheat oven to 350°. Line a 13-in. x 9-in. x 2-in. baking pan with foil. Generously grease foil.

In a medium bowl, whisk together the flour and next five ingredients.

Melt butter and brown sugar in a heavy saucepan over medium low heat. Cool slightly. Quickly whisk in egg and vanilla–if butter mixture is still too hot, the egg will start to cook when added. If this happens, keep whisking quickly and the cooked egg should break up and no longer be noticeable.

Transfer butter mixture to a medium bowl. Whisk in the flour mixture. Stir in toffee pieces, ½ cup of the coconut, ½ cup of the pecans and the chocolate chips.

Spread into prepared pan.

Sprinkle remaining coconut and pecans over the top of the batter and press firmly into batter.

Bake for 20-25 minutes or until center is set. Let cool in pan on wire rack.

When brownies are completely cooled, lift foil liner out of pan and cut into bars. For best results, clean knife off with hot water after each cut.

Yield: 12-18 bars

Fudgy Oat Bars

2 cups GF oats
1 ½ cups GF all-purpose baking flour
1 cup packed brown sugar
¾ teaspoon salt
³/₈ teaspoon xanthan gum
1 cup (2 sticks) butter, melted
1 cup chopped pecans
1 can (14 ounces) sweetened condensed milk
1 cup semi-sweet chocolate chips
2 tablespoons shortening
1 cup plain M&M's®

Preheat oven to 350°. Grease or foil line and grease a 13-in. x 9-in. x 2-in. baking pan.

In a large bowl, combine the oats and next four ingredients. Add butter and mix until crumbly. Stir in pecans. Set aside 1 ½ cups for topping. Press remaining crumb mixture into prepared pan.

In a saucepan, combine the milk, chocolate chips and shortening; cook and stir over low heat until chips are melted. Spread over crust; sprinkle with the reserved crumb mixture. Top with M&M's.

Bake for 20-25 minutes or until edges are golden brown.

Yield: 2 ½ dozen bars

"Absolutely eat dessert first."
—Joss Whedon

Peanut Butter Chip Bars

⅔ cup butter
⅔ cup peanut butter*
1 cup granulated sugar
1 cup packed brown sugar
4 eggs
2 teaspoons vanilla extract
2 cups GF all-purpose baking flour
2 teaspoons baking powder
1 teaspoon xanthan gum
½ teaspoon salt
1 package (12 ounces) chocolate chips, milk or semi-sweet

Preheat oven to 350°. Grease or foil line and grease a 13-in. x 9-in. x 2-in. baking pan.

In a large bowl, cream the butter and next 3 ingredients. Add eggs, one at a time, beating well after each addition. Beat in vanilla.

In a separate bowl, whisk together the flour and next three ingredients; gradually add to creamed mixture. Stir in chocolate chips.

Spread in prepared baking pan and bake for 45-50 minutes or until a toothpick inserted near the center comes out clean.

Cool on wire rack. Cut into bars.

Yield: 2 dozen

*Recipe was tested using Smart Balance peanut butter
Lindy's note: I have found Smart Balance peanut butter is the best and peanut-iest tasting peanut butter for baking.

"Peanut butter and chocolate... That's pretty much the greatest invention of the last century."
-Tom Lenk

Polka Dotted Brownies

1 ¾ cups GF all-purpose baking flour
¾ teaspoon baking powder
¾ teaspoon xanthan gum
¾ teaspoon salt
½ cup (1 stick) butter
4 ounces unsweetened chocolate
1 ½ cups granulated sugar
4 eggs
1 teaspoon vanilla extract

CHEESECAKE BATTER:
6 ounces cream cheese, softened
⅓ cup GF all-purpose baking flour
½ cup granulated sugar
½ teaspoon vanilla extract
2 tablespoons milk

Preheat oven to 350°. Line a 13-in. x 9-in. x 2-in. baking pan with foil and grease well.

BROWNIE BATTER:

In a medium bowl, whisk together the flour and next three ingredients.

Melt butter and chocolate in the top of a double boiler or in a microwave safe bowl, stirring often until smooth. If using the microwave, stir every 30 seconds until chocolate is almost melted.

Add sugar to chocolate mixture; stir to combine. Add eggs and vanilla; stir until smooth. Stir in flour mixture until just combined. Spoon into prepared pan; spread evenly.

CHEESECAKE BATTER:

In a medium mixing bowl, beat cream cheese until smooth. On low speed, beat in flour, sugar and vanilla. Add milk; mix until smooth.

With a spoon or small cookie scoop, dollop batter on top of brownie batter in an uneven pattern. (The cheesecake mounds will flatten as it bakes.)

Bake for 30 minutes or until firm to the touch and set.

Cool completely on wire rack.

Lift foil from pan and cut into squares.

Yield: 24 brownies

Raspberry Chocolate Bars

1 ½ cups GF all-purpose baking flour
1 ½ cups GF oats
½ cup granulated sugar
½ cup packed brown sugar
½ teaspoon xanthan gum
¼ teaspoon salt
1 cup (2 sticks) cold butter, cubed
¾ cup seedless raspberry jam
2 cups semi-sweet chocolate chips*
¼ cup chopped walnuts

Preheat oven to 375°. Grease or foil line and grease a 9-in. square baking dish.

In a large bowl, whisk together the flour and next five ingredients. Cut in butter until mixture resembles coarse crumbs. Set aside 1 cup for topping. Press remaining mixture into prepared baking pan. Spread with jam; sprinkle with chocolate chips.

In a medium bowl, combine the walnuts and reserved crumb mixture; sprinkle over top of chocolate chips.

Bake for 30-35 minutes or until lightly browned and bubbly.

Cool on wire rack. Cut into squares.

Yield: 16 squares

*Recipe was tested using 1 cup semi-sweet chocolate chips and 1 cup 60% bittersweet chocolate chips

Did you know?

Raspberries contain 40% of your daily needs for Vitamin C.

Todd's Brownies

2 cups granulated sugar
¾ cup baking cocoa
1 cup canola oil
4 eggs
¼ cup milk
1 ½ cups GF all-purpose baking flour
1 teaspoon salt
1 teaspoon baking powder
¾ teaspoon xanthan gum
1 cup semi-sweet chocolate chips
1 cup chopped peanuts, *divided*
1 package (14 ounces) caramels*
1 can (14 ounces) sweetened condensed milk

Preheat oven to 350°. Line 13-in. x 9-in. x 2-in. baking pan with foil and grease bottom and sides well.

In a large mixing bowl, beat the sugar, and next four ingredients until well mixed.

In another bowl, whisk together the flour and next three ingredients; gradually add to egg mixture until well blended. Fold in chocolate chips and ½ cup peanuts.

Spoon two-thirds of the batter into prepared pan. Bake for 12-14 minutes or until almost set.

In a large saucepan, heat the caramels and condensed milk over low heat until caramels are melted. Pour caramel mixture over baked brownie layer. Sprinkle with remaining peanuts.

Drop remaining batter by tablespoonfuls over caramel layer; carefully swirl brownie batter with a knife.

Bake 35-40 minutes longer or until a toothpick inserted near the center comes out with moist crumbs (do not over bake). Cool on wire rack.

Lift foil from pan and cut into squares.**

Yield: 24 brownies

*Recipe was tested using Kraft Caramel Bits
**Heat large knife up under hot water to ease in cutting. Clean knife after each cut with hot water.

Wonder Bars

2 ¼ cups GF all-purpose baking flour, *divided*
2 cups GF oats
1 ½ cups packed brown sugar
1 teaspoon baking soda
1 teaspoon xanthan gum
½ teaspoon salt
1 ½ cups (3 sticks) cold butter, cubed
1 cup (6 ounces) semi-sweet chocolate chips
1 cup (6 ounces) 60% bittersweet chocolate chips
1 jar (12 ounces) caramel ice cream topping

Preheat oven to 350°. Grease or foil line and grease a 13-in. x 9-in. x 2-in. baking pan.

In a large bowl, combine 2 cups of flour and the next five ingredients. Cut in butter until crumbly.

Press half of crumb mixture into prepared pan and bake for 15 minutes.

Take pan out of oven and sprinkle chocolate chips over the crust.

In a medium bowl, whisk together the caramel topping and remaining ¼ cup flour until smooth; drizzle over chocolate chips.

Sprinkle remaining crumb mixture over caramel layer and bake for 20-25 minutes or until golden brown.

Cool completely on wire rack.

Lift foil from pan and cut into squares.*

Yield: 2 dozen

*Heat large knife up under hot water to ease in cutting. Clean knife after each cut with hot water.

> **"Never lose childlike wonder."**
> *-Randy Pausch*

Frosted Zucchini Brownies

BROWNIES:
8 ounces zucchini*, cut into chunks
3 tablespoons butter, melted
3 large eggs
1 teaspoon vanilla extract
¾ cup granulated sugar
⅔ cup unsweetened baking cocoa
½ teaspoon baking powder
¼ teaspoon salt, heaping
¼ teaspoon xanthan gum
½ cup all-purpose GF baking flour
¾ cup semi-sweet chocolate chips
¾ cup chopped walnuts (optional)

*If you do not have a food scale, 8 ounces is about 1 ½ cups shredded zucchini lightly packed down.

FROSTING:
¾ cup semi-sweet chocolate chips
3 tablespoons milk

Preheat oven to 350°. Lightly spray a 9" square baking pan with cooking oil.

Brownies: Combine the zucchini, butter, eggs and vanilla in the bowl of a food processor and process until smooth.

Add the sugar and next five ingredients. Pulse until just combined (I only had to pulse 3 times to get ingredients to just combine.)

Add the chips and nuts (if desired) and pulse 2-3 more times.

Pour batter into prepared baking pan and place in center of oven.

Bake for 25-30 minutes or until a toothpick inserted into the center comes out clean, or with a few moist crumbs. Continue baking if any wet batter shows up on toothpick.

Remove brownies from oven and allow to cool completely before frosting.

Frosting: Combine the chocolate chips and milk in heavy saucepan. Heat and stir until chips begin to soften. Remove from heat and whisk until frosting is smooth.

Spread frosting on brownies and refrigerate for 1 hour to set frosting. Store at room temperature, covered.

These will keep for several days on your kitchen counter (if they last that long!). IF there are any left after a few days, cut up the remaining brownies and wrap individually. Place in freezer zip lock type bag and freeze.

Breads & Muffins

Did you know? Sliced bread was invented in 1928 and referred to as the best thing since bagged bread.

Muffins are a snack staple for me—brunch snack, before dinner snack, fishing boat snack....you get the idea. And for some crazy reason, I will eat muffins before slicing into a loaf of sweet bread—even if it is the same recipe, just a different shape. Call me crazy!

Enjoy these perfectly "sweet" breads & muffins!

Apple Nut Muffins
Carol's Spicy Zucchini Bread
Chocolate Chip Zucchini Muffins
Double Chocolate Pumpkin Bread
Give Thanks Muffins
Cinnamon Raisin Bread
Lemon Blueberry Biscuits
Peanut Streusel Bread
Pumpkin Apple Muffins
Strawberry Bread with Berry Spread
New Blueberry Muffins
Ping's Pumpkin Bread
Lemon Zucchini Bread
Ginger Cranberry Muffins
Dutch Apple Bread

Apple Nut Muffins

FILLING:
1 tablespoon butter
2 ½ tablespoons packed brown sugar
1 ½ teaspoon GF all-purpose baking flour
½ teaspoon ground cinnamon
¼ teaspoon ground nutmeg
1 cup finely chopped peeled apples
⅓ cup finely chopped walnuts

MUFFINS:
6 tablespoons butter, softened
¾ cup granulated sugar
2 eggs
¾ teaspoon vanilla extract
1 ¾ cups GF all-purpose baking flour
1 ¼ teaspoon xanthan gum
¾ teaspoon baking powder
¾ teaspoon baking soda
½ teaspoon cinnamon
¾ cup sour cream

TOPPING:
1 tablespoon granulated sugar
1 teaspoon ground cinnamon

Grease or paper-line 12-cup muffin pan.

In a sauce pan, melt butter. Stir in brown sugar, and next three ingredients until smooth. Add apples and cook over medium-low heat for 10 minutes or until apples are tender, stirring frequently. Remove from heat and stir in nuts. Set aside to cool.

Preheat oven to 350°.

In a large mixing bowl, cream together butter and sugar. Add eggs, one at a time, beating well after each addition. Beat in vanilla.

In medium bowl, whisk together the flour and next four ingredients. Add to the creamed mixture alternately with the sour cream.

Spoon a couple tablespoons of batter into prepared muffin cups. Place a spoonful of apple mixture into the center of each cup of batter – do not spread the apple mixture around the cup.

Carefully spoon more batter into each cup, covering the apple mixture.

In a small bowl, mix the cinnamon and sugar together, sprinkle over the muffins.

Bake for 15-20 minutes or until a toothpick inserted in the center comes out clean. Cool 5 minutes before removing from pans to wire rack.

Yield: 1 dozen

Carol's Spicy Zucchini Bread

3 cups GF all-purpose baking flour
2 ¼ teaspoons xanthan gum
2 teaspoons ground cinnamon
1 teaspoon ground nutmeg
1 teaspoon baking powder
1 teaspoon baking soda
½ teaspoon salt
1 cup chopped pecans
¾ cup vegetable oil
3 eggs
2 cups granulated sugar
2 teaspoons vanilla extract
3 cups unpeeled shredded zucchini (2 medium zucchini)

Preheat oven to 350°. Grease two 9-in. x 5-in. loaf pans.

In a large bowl, whisk together the flour and next seven ingredients. Make a well in center of mixture.

In a medium bowl, combine oil and next three ingredients. Stir in zucchini. Add zucchini mixture to dry ingredients, stirring just until moistened.

Spoon batter into prepared loaf pans.

Bake for 1 hour or until wooden pick inserted into center comes out clean.

Cool loaves 10 minutes on wire rack. Remove from pans to cool completely.

These freeze well.

Did you know?

April 25th is National Zucchini Bread Day. It's also my daughter's birthday. :)

Chocolate Chip Zucchini Muffins

1 ½ cups GF all-purpose baking flour
¾ cup granulated sugar
1 rounded teaspoon ground cinnamon
1 teaspoon xanthan gum
1 teaspoon baking soda
½ teaspoon salt
½ cup vegetable oil
¼ cup milk
1 egg, lightly beaten
1 tablespoon lemon juice
1 teaspoon vanilla extract
1 cup shredded zucchini
1 cup semi-sweet chocolate chips

Grease or paper-line a 12-cup muffin pan.

Preheat oven to 350°.

In a large bowl, whisk together the flour and next five ingredients.

In measuring cup for liquids or small bowl, combine the oil and next four ingredients; mix well.

Add to flour mixture, stir until just moistened.

Fold in zucchini and chocolate chips.

Fill prepared muffin pan two-thirds full. Bake for 20-25 minutes or until a wooden pick inserted in the center comes out clean.

Yield: 12 muffins

Did you know?

Chocolate chips were created by accident by Ruth Graves Wakefield of Toll House Inn in 1937.

Double Chocolate Pumpkin Bread

3 ½ cups granulated sugar
¾ cup vegetable oil*
½ cup applesauce
3 eggs
1 can (29 ounces) pumpkin
4 ounces unsweetened chocolate, melted and cooled
1 ½ teaspoon vanilla extract
3 ¾ cups GF all-purpose baking flour
2 ¼ teaspoons xanthan gum
1 ½ teaspoons salt
1 ½ teaspoons baking powder
1 ¼ teaspoons baking soda
1 ¼ teaspoons ground cinnamon
1 ¼ teaspoons ground cloves
½ teaspoon ground nutmeg
2 cups (12 ounces) semi-sweet chocolate chips

Preheat oven to 350°. Grease 8 - 5 ¾" x 3" loaf pans.**

In a large mixing bowl, beat together sugar, oil and applesauce. Add eggs and mix well. Add the pumpkin, chocolate and vanilla; mix well.

In a separate bowl, whisk together the flour and next 7 ingredients. Using a spoon, stir into the pumpkin mixture just until blended. Stir in chocolate chips.

Spoon batter into prepared loaf pans and bake for 50-55 minutes or until toothpick inserted in center comes out clean.

Cool on wire rack for 10 minutes before removing from pans to cool completely.

Wrap in plastic wrap and then again in foil. These freeze very well.

*Recipe was tested using canola oil
. **3 9-in. x 5-in. loaf pans may be used instead of small loaf pans. Bake for 55-65 minutes or until toothpick inserted in center comes out clean.

Give Thanks Muffins

1 cup canned pumpkin
2 large eggs
½ cup firmly packed brown sugar
3 tablespoons canola oil
1 tablespoon molasses
1 rounded teaspoon ground cinnamon
½ teaspoon salt
¼ teaspoon ground cloves
¼ teaspoon ground ginger
½ cup milk
1 cup dried cranberries
1 cup cinnamon chips
1 ½ cup GF all-purpose flour
1 ⅛ teaspoon xanthan gum
1 teaspoon baking powder
½ teaspoon baking soda
Coarse sugar for topping, optional

Grease or paper-line 12-cup muffin pan.

In a large bowl whisk together the pumpkin and next 9 ingredients, making sure sides and bottom of bowl are well scraped. Stir in cranberries and cinnamon chips.

In a separate bowl, whisk together the flour and next 3 ingredients. Add to pumpkin mixture and mix well.

Cover the bowl and let batter rest for 30 minutes.

Preheat oven to 400°.

Fill each muffin cup 2/3 full. Sprinkle with coarse sugar if desired. Bake for 15-20 minutes or until a toothpick inserted in the center comes out clean.

Cool on wire rack.

Yield: 12-16 muffins

"Greet every morning with open arms and say thanks every night with a full heart."
-Regina Brett

Cinnamon Raisin Bread

2 cups GF all-purpose baking flour
1 cup granulated sugar, **divided**
1 ½ teaspoon xanthan gum
1 teaspoons baking soda
½ teaspoon salt
1 egg
1 cup buttermilk
¼ cup canola oil
½ cup raisins
1 ½ teaspoons ground cinnamon

Preheat oven to 350°. Grease one 9-in.x 5-in. loaf pan.

In a large bowl, whisk together the flour, ¾ cup sugar, and next three ingredients.

In a small bowl, whisk together the eggs, buttermilk and oil. Stir into dry ingredients just until moistened. Fold in raisins.

Combine cinnamon and remaining sugar; set aside.

Spoon half of the batter into prepared pan. Sprinkle with half of the reserved cinnamon-sugar mixture; spoon remaining batter over cinnamon-sugar layer. Sprinkle with remaining cinnamon-sugar. Cut through batter with a knife to swirl.

Bake for 55-60 minutes or until a toothpick inserted near the center comes out clean.

Cool in pan for 10 minutes before removing from pans to wire racks.

Yield: 1 loaf

Did you know?
In Ancient Egypt, cinnamon was once valued more than gold.

Lemon Blueberry Biscuits

2 cups GF all-purpose baking flour
½ cup granulated sugar
2 teaspoons baking powder
1 teaspoon xanthan gum
½ teaspoon baking soda
¼ teaspoon salt
1 cup (8 ounces) vanilla yogurt
1 tablespoon fresh lemon juice
1 egg, lightly beaten
1 teaspoon grated lemon peel
1 cup fresh or frozen blueberries*

GLAZE:
½ cup powdered sugar
1 tablespoon lemon juice
½ teaspoon grated lemon peel

Preheat oven to 400°. Grease or paper-line 12-cup muffin pan.

In a large bowl, whisk together the flour and next five ingredients.

In a small bowl, combine the yogurt and next three ingredients; stir into dry ingredients just until moistened. Fold in blueberries.

Fill prepared muffin cups 2/3 full. Bake for 15 minutes or until lightly browned.

In a small bowl, combine glaze ingredients; drizzle over warm biscuits.

Yield: 1 dozen

*If using frozen blueberries, do not thaw before adding to batter.

> "When life gives you a lemon, take it. Don't waste food."
> –Giselle Marquez

Peanut Streusel Bread

STREUSEL TOPPING:
1 cup dry-roasted salted peanuts
½ cup GF all-purpose baking flour
¼ cup (½ stick) butter, melted
3 tablespoons firmly packed brown sugar
2 tablespoons granulated sugar
⅛ teaspoon salt

In a medium bowl, combine all ingredients. Let stand 15 minutes or until mixture is firm. Crumble into small pieces.

BREAD:
1 egg
1 cup firmly packed brown sugar
2 tablespoons creamy peanut butter
2 tablespoons butter, melted
2 cups GF all-purpose baking flour
1 ½ teaspoons xanthan gum
1 teaspoon baking powder
½ teaspoon baking soda
½ teaspoon salt
1 cup buttermilk

Preheat oven to 350°.

Line bottom and sides of a 9-in. x 5 in. loaf pan with heavy-duty aluminum foil, allowing 2 to 3 inches to extend over sides.

In a mixing bowl, beat egg and sugar at medium speed for 2 minutes or until creamy; add peanut butter and butter, beating until blended.

In a separate bowl, whisk together the flour and next four ingredients.

Whisk in egg mixture and buttermilk just until blended. (Batter will be slightly lumpy.)

Spoon about 2/3 cup peanut streusel topping on bottom of prepared pan. Spoon half of batter over streusel, carefully spreading batter over streusel and gently spreading batter to sides of pan over streusel. Repeat this one more time.

Sprinkle remaining 2/3 cup peanut streusel topping over batter, gently pressing topping into batter.

Bake for 1 hour or until a long wooden pick inserted in center comes out clean.

Shield with foil after 45 minutes if necessary.

Cool in pan on a wire rack 10 minutes.

Lift loaf from pan, using foil sides as handles. Place loaf on a wire rack. Carefully pull down sides of foil; cool completely.

Pumpkin Apple Muffins

2 ½ cups GF all-purpose flour
2 scant teaspoons xanthan gum
2 cups granulated sugar
1 tablespoon pumpkin pie spice
1 teaspoon baking soda
½ teaspoon salt
2 eggs
1 cup canned or cooked pumpkin
½ cup vegetable oil
2 cups finely chopped peeled apples

STREUSEL:
¼ cup granulated sugar
2 tablespoons GF all-purpose flour
1 tablespoon ground cinnamon
4 teaspoons cold butter or margarine

Preheat oven to 350°. Grease or paper-line 12-cup and 6-cup muffin pan.

In a bowl, whisk together the first six ingredients.

In another bowl, combine the eggs, pumpkin, and oil; stir into dry ingredients just until moistened. Fold in apples. Fill prepared muffin pan two-thirds full.

In a small bowl, combine sugar, flour and cinnamon. Cut in butter until crumbly. Sprinkle over batter.

Bake for 20-25 minutes or until golden brown and a toothpick inserted in the center comes out clean.

Cool for 5 minutes before removing from pans to wire racks.

Yield: 1½ dozen

> "You can't celebrate Fall without its leading role... pumpkin!"
> –Giselle Marquez

Strawberry Bread with Berry Spread

BERRY SPREAD:

In a small mixing bowl, beat cream cheese until smooth. Drain strawberries, reserving ¼ cup of juice for the bread batter. Add 6 tablespoons of berries to the cream cheese; beat well. Set remaining berries aside for bread.

Chill spread until ready to serve.

BREAD:

Preheat oven to 350°. Grease two 8-in.x4-in. loaf pans.

In a large bowl, whisk together the flour and next four ingredients.

In a medium bowl, whisk together the eggs, oil, remaining berries, and juice. Stir into dry ingredients just until moistened. Carefully work out any pockets of flour. Fold in nuts.

(Batter will be stiff).

Transfer batter to prepared loaf pans and bake for 50-55 minutes or until a toothpick inserted near the center comes out clean.

Cool in pans on wire rack for 10 minutes before removing from pans to cool completely.

Yield: 2 loaves, about 1 cup spread

1 package (8 ounces) cream cheese, softened
2 packages (10 ounces each) frozen sweetened sliced strawberries, thawed
3 cups GF all-purpose baking flour
2 cups granulated sugar
2 ¼ teaspoons xanthan gum
1 teaspoon salt
1 teaspoon baking soda
4 eggs
1 cup canola oil
1 cup chopped walnuts, optional

New Blueberry Muffins

½ cup (1 stick) butter, softened
1 cup granulated sugar
2 eggs
1 cup (8 ounces) vanilla yogurt
1 teaspoon vanilla extract
2 cups GF all-purpose baking flour, sifted
1 ½ teaspoons xanthan gum
1 teaspoon baking soda
1 rounded teaspoon ground cinnamon
½ teaspoon baking powder
½ teaspoon salt
¼ teaspoon ground nutmeg
1 ½ cups fresh or frozen blueberries*

TOPPING:
1 tablespoon sugar
1 teaspoon ground cinnamon

Preheat oven to 375°. Grease or paper-line a 12-cup and one cup in a 6-cup muffin pan.

In a large mixing bowl, cream butter and sugar. Add eggs, one at a time, beating well after each addition. Add yogurt and vanilla; mix well.

In a separate bowl, whisk together flour and next six ingredients. Stir into creamed mixture just until moistened. Fold in blueberries. Fill prepared muffin cups full.

Combine topping ingredients; sprinkle over batter.

Bake for 20-30 minutes or until a toothpick inserted near the center comes out clean.

Cool for 5 minutes before removing from the pans to wire racks.

Yield: 13 muffins

*If using frozen blueberries, do not thaw before adding to batter.

Did you know?

A single blueberry bush can produce as many as 6,000 blueberries per year.

Ping's Pumpkin Bread

2 ½ cups GF all-purpose baking flour
3 cups granulated sugar
2 teaspoons ground cinnamon, rounded
2 teaspoons ground nutmeg
2 teaspoons baking soda
1 ¾ teaspoons xanthan gum
1 ½ teaspoons salt
²/₃ cup cold water
½ cup canola oil
½ cup applesauce
1 teaspoon vanilla extract
1 – 15 oz. can pumpkin
4 eggs, lightly beaten

Preheat oven to 350°.

Grease 2 - 9"x5" loaf pans.

In a large mixing bowl whisk together flour and next six ingredients. Using a large spoon, make a well in the flour mixture.

Add the water and remaining next five ingredients; mix well.

Pour batter into prepared pans.

Bake for 1 hour or until toothpick inserted in center comes out mostly clean.

Cool for 45 minutes and carefully remove from pans. Cool completely. Wrap in plastic wrap and foil. These freeze well.

Yield: 2 loaves

> "Make pumpkin bread the default gift for everyone. It's cheap, it's beloved, it's carbs."
> –Karen Bender

Lemon Zucchini Bread

1 ²/₃ cup GF all-purpose baking flour
2 teaspoons baking powder
1 ¼ teaspoons xanthan gum
½ teaspoon salt
¾ cup granulated sugar
2 tablespoons lemon zest*
½ cup canola oil
2 large eggs, room temperature
¼ cup sour cream
1 ½ teaspoons fresh lemon juice
1 cup finely grated zucchini
Glaze:
1 cup powdered sugar
1 ½ - 2 tablespoons fresh lemon juice
1 tablespoon lemon zest* (optional)

Preheat oven to 350°. Butter or spray with cooking oil an 8 by 4-inch loaf pan. If using butter, dust pan with a light coating of flour and tap out the excess.

In a medium bowl, whisk together the flour and next three ingredients.

In a separate medium bowl, beat (with electric mixer) the sugar and lemon zest for 30 seconds.

In liquid measuring cup, whisk together the oil and eggs until well combined, add to sugar mixture and mix well.

Add about half the flour mixture to the sugar mixture and mix until just combined.

Add the sour cream and lemon juice, mix until just combined, add remaining flour mixture and mix until some flour remains to be incorporated.

Add zucchini and stir in with large spoon. Batter will be thick.

Pour batter into prepared pan and bake for 45-50 minutes or until toothpick inserted near the center comes out clean.

Cool in pan on a wire rack for 10 minutes. Remove loaf from pan to cool completely.

Once loaf is almost cooled, pour glaze over bread.

Glaze: In a small bowl, mix together the sugar and juice until desired consistency is achieved. Add zest if desired. Drizzle over loaf – enjoy!

*I zested 2 small lemons and had plenty of zest for the loaf and more than a tablespoon left over so I decided to add that to the glaze

Ginger Cranberry Muffins

2 ¼ cups GF all-purpose baking flour
½ cup brown sugar, packed
2 teaspoons ground ginger
1 ½ teaspoons xanthan gum
1 teaspoon baking powder
1 teaspoon ground cinnamon, rounded
¾ teaspoon salt
½ teaspoon baking soda
1 egg
¾ cup water
½ cup sour cream
⅓ cup molasses
¼ cup canola oil
1 cup dried cranberries

Preheat oven to 350°. Coat 12 cup muffin pan with cooking spray.

In a large bowl, combine flour and next seven ingredients.

In a small bowl or 2 cup liquid measuring cup, combine the egg and next four ingredients.

Stir into dry ingredients just until moistened. Fold in cranberries.

Fill each cup ¾ full with batter.

Bake for 18-22 minutes or until a toothpick comes out clean.

Cool 5 minutes before removing from pan to a wire rack to cool.

Yield: 1 dozen

Did you know?

Ginger is actually a rhizome (an underground stem), not a root.

Dutch Apple Bread

½ cup (1 stick) butter
1 cup granulated sugar
2 eggs
1 teaspoon vanilla extract
2 cups GF all-purpose baking flour
1 ½ teaspoons xanthan gum
1 teaspoon baking soda
1 teaspoon ground cinnamon
½ teaspoon salt
¼ teaspoon ground nutmeg
⅓ cup buttermilk
1 cup chopped peeled apples
⅓ cup chopped walnuts
TOPPING:
⅓ cup GF all-purpose baking flour
2 tablespoons granulated sugar
2 tablespoons packed brown sugar
1 teaspoon ground cinnamon
3 tablespoons cold butter

Preheat oven to 350°. Grease 4 - 5 ¾" x 3" loaf pans*.

In a large mixing bowl, cream butter and sugar until fluffy. Beat in eggs, one at a time; add vanilla, mix well.

In a medium bowl, whisk together flour and next five ingredients; stir into the creamed mixture alternately with buttermilk.

Fold in apple and nuts.

Pour into prepared loaf pans.

For topping, combine the first four ingredients; cut in butter until crumbly. Sprinkle over batter.

Bake for 30-35 minutes or until toothpick inserted near the middle comes out clean.

Cool in pan on wire rack for 10 minutes before removing from pan to cool completely.

*1 - 9-in. x 5-in. loaf pans may be used instead of small loaf pans. Bake for 55-65 minutes or until toothpick inserted in center comes out clean.

Cakes & Cupcakes

> "You cannot have a cake and eat it too. Either you eat it, or you have it."
> —Zygmunt Bauman

I really do not know what is more fun to eat–a cookie or a cupcake! In this section you'll find so many variations on the all famous cupcakes and cakes. It was very difficult to decide which recipes to publish first. You will find some of my absolute favorites in these pages. The Chocolate Sour Cream Cake has become my favorite "go to" chocolate cake. I make it as a layer cake for birthdays and as cupcakes for fun snacks. I find that cupcakes are also easier to freeze than slices of cake. A trick I use often is to make the cupcakes ahead of time and freeze them–unfrosted. When the time to serve them gets closer–even same day–take them out of the freezer, make the frosting, and then frost. Cakes are much easier to frost when frozen, just make sure you leave enough time for the cake to thaw before serving–unless you like to eat frozen treats and these are great either way!

As a side note–when baking anything chocolate, I always make it at least one day ahead so the chocolate can 'age'. When baking cake layers, after the layers have cooled completely, wrap in plastic wrap, then foil–place in freezer. I find if I can bake 2-3 days ahead and freeze, then take it out of freezer, make the frosting and frost–the cake is not just good, but really, really good!!

Watch out for these delectible desserts!

Almost Totally Free Cupcakes
Chocolate Cream Cheese Cupcakes
Beverly's Lemon Pound Cake
Banana Cupcakes
Chocolate Sour Cream Cake
Old Fashioned Crumb Cake
Chocolate Peanut Surprise Cupcakes
Spiced Zucchini Cupcakes with Caramel Frosting
Cream Filled Carrot Cake
Red Velvet Cupcakes
Pineapple Cake with Pecan-Coconut Frosting
Cinnamon-Caramel Cupcakes
Mexican Cake
Apple Cake with Caramel Sauce
Texas Sheet Cake

Almost Totally Free Chocolate Cupcakes

1 ½ cups GF all-purpose baking flour
1 cup granulated sugar
3 tablespoons baking cocoa, heaping
1 teaspoon baking soda
¾ teaspoon xanthan gum
½ teaspoon salt
¼ teaspoon ground cinnamon
6 tablespoons vegetable oil
1 teaspoon white vinegar
1 teaspoon vanilla extract
1 cup cold water

DAIRY FREE CHOCOLATE FROSTING:
1 cup butter flavored shortening
2 teaspoons vanilla extract
1 cup baking cocoa
3-4 cups powdered sugar
4-6 tablespoons almond or coconut milk

Preheat oven to 350°. Paper line 12 cup muffin pan.

In a large mixing bowl, whisk together flour and next six ingredients.

Use a spoon to make three wells in the dry mixture. Pour oil in one, vinegar into second and vanilla into the last one. Slowly pour water over all. Beat together using low speed until completely combined. The batter will be thin.

Pour batter into prepared pan.

Bake for 15-20 minutes or until a toothpick inserted near center comes out clean.

Cool on wire rack.

FROSTING:

In a medium mixing bowl, beat shortening and vanilla until fluffy.

Gradually add cocoa, beating well.

Gradually add 1 cup powdered sugar and 2 tablespoons milk, beat well. Continue to add sugar and milk until desired spreading consistency is obtained.

Frost cupcakes.

Yield: 12 cupcakes

Chocolate Cream Cheese Cupcakes

1 package (8 ounces) cream cheese
1 ½ cups granulated sugar, *divided*
1 egg
1 teaspoon salt, *divided*
1 cup (6 ounces) semisweet chocolate chips
1 ½ cups GF all-purpose flour
⅓ cup baking cocoa
1 teaspoon baking soda
¾ teaspoon xanthan gum
1 cup water
⅓ cup canola oil
1 tablespoon white vinegar

FROSTING:
3 ½ cups powdered sugar
3 tablespoons baking cocoa
½ cup butter, melted
6 tablespoons milk
1 teaspoon vanilla extract
Chopped pecans (optional)

For cream cheese filling, in a small bowl, beat cream cheese and ½ cup sugar until smooth. Beat in egg and ½ teaspoon salt until combined. Fold in chocolate chips; set aside.

Preheat oven to 350°. Grease or paper-line one 12-cup muffin pan and one 6-cup muffin pan.

In a large bowl, whisk together the flour, cocoa, baking soda, and remaining sugar and salt. In a small bowl, whisk together the water, oil and vinegar. Stir into dry ingredients just until moistened.

Fill prepared muffin cups half full with batter. Drop filling by heaping tablespoonfuls into the center of each cup. Bake for 25-30 minutes or until a toothpick inserted in cake comes out clean. Cool for 10 minutes before removing from pans to wire racks to cool completely.

For frosting, in a large bowl, combine the powdered sugar and next four ingredients. Beat until blended. Frost cupcakes; sprinkle with pecans if desired.

Yield: 18 cupcakes

Beverly's Lemon Pound Cake

1 cup (2 sticks) butter, no substitutes
½ cup shortening*
3 cups granulated sugar
6 eggs
3 cups GF all-purpose baking flour
1 ½ teaspoons xanthan gum
1 teaspoon salt
½ teaspoon baking powder
1 cup sour cream
¼ cup milk
2 teaspoons lemon extract
1 teaspoon vanilla extract

OPTIONAL GLAZE:
1 cup powdered sugar**
2 tablespoons fresh lemon juice
1 teaspoon grated lemon peel

Preheat oven to 325°. Grease 12-cup bundt pan.

In a large mixing bowl, cream together the butter, shortening and sugar until fluffy.

Add eggs, one at a time, beating well after each addition.

In a separate mixing bowl, whisk together the flour and next three ingredients.

In a small bowl, mix together the sour cream, milk and flavorings. Add flour mixture and sour cream mixture alternately to creamed mixture ending with sour cream mixture.

Pour batter into prepared pan. Bake for 1 hour and 15 minutes to 1 hour and 30 minutes or until wooden pick inserted in the center of cake comes out clean.

Cool for 15 minutes on wire rack. Remove from pan.

If desired, prepare glaze while cake is cooling.

Combine all glaze ingredients in small bowl. Drizzle over warm cake.

*Recipe was tested using organic shortening
**More or less sugar can be used according to taste preference

Banana Cupcakes

½ cup shortening*
1 ½ cups granulated sugar
2 eggs
1 cup mashed ripe bananas (about 2 medium)
1 teaspoon vanilla extract
2 cups GF all-purpose baking flour
1 teaspoon xanthan gum
¾ teaspoon baking soda
½ teaspoon baking powder
½ teaspoon salt
½ teaspoon ground cinnamon
½ cup buttermilk**

FROSTING:
2 cups powdered sugar
1/3 cup (5 1/3 tablespoons) butter, softened
3 tablespoons mashed ripe banana
1 tablespoon lemon juice
1 tablespoon milk, more or less for desired spreading consistency

Preheat oven to 375°. Paper-line muffin cups.

In a large mixing bowl, cream shortening and sugar until light and fluffy. Add eggs, one at a time, beating well after each addition. Beat in bananas and vanilla.

In another large bowl, whisk together the flour and next five ingredients. Gradually add to creamed mixture alternately with buttermilk, beating well after each addition.

Fill prepared muffin cups two-thirds full. Bake for 18-22 minutes or until a toothpick inserted near the center comes out clean. Cool for 10 minutes before removing from pan to a wire rack to cool completely.

In a small mixing bowl, combine one cup of powdered sugar and butter. Add mashed banana and lemon juice, mix well. Carefully add the remaining one cup of powdered sugar. Add milk as needed to achieve desired spreading consistency.

Frost cooled cupcakes.

Yield: 22 cupcakes

*Recipe was tested using organic shortening
**Recipe was tested using buttermilk powder, prepared via package directions.

Chocolate Sour Cream Cake

¾ cup canola oil
1 egg
2 teaspoons vanilla extract
1 cup firmly packed brown sugar
½ cup granulated sugar
2 ounces semi-sweet baking chocolate, melted
2 cups GF all-purpose baking flour
⅔ cup unsweetened baking cocoa
1 tablespoon baking soda
1 teaspoon xanthan gum
½ teaspoon salt
1 cup warm water
1 cup sour cream

FROSTING:
½ cup (1 stick) butter, softened
⅔ cup baking cocoa
1 teaspoon vanilla extract
¼ cup sour cream
¼ cup milk
2-3 cups powdered sugar

Preheat oven to 350°. Grease and flour two 8-inch baking pans.

In a large mixing bowl beat together oil, egg and vanilla for 1 minute. Add sugars; beat until well mixed, about 1 minute. Add melted chocolate; continue beating, making sure sides of bowl are scraped down often. Beat for 1 more minute.

In a small bowl, whisk together flour and next four ingredients. Add flour mixture to chocolate mixture alternately with water, beating well after each addition. Add sour cream and mix well.

Pour batter into prepared pans and bake for 30-35 minutes or until a wooden pick inserted into center comes out clean.

Cool pans on wire rack for 10 minutes. Remove cakes from pans to cool completely.

Prepare frosting while cakes are cooling.

In a large mixing bowl, beat butter at high speed until creamy, about 1-2 minutes. Add cocoa and vanilla, beat until creamy; 1-2 minutes. Add 1 cup powdered sugar, beat well. Add sour cream and milk; beat until creamy. Add enough sugar for desired spreading consistency. Beat until creamy.

Place one cake, flat side up, on bottom of plate. Place about 1 cup frosting in center of cake. Spread to about 1/2-in. from edge of cake. Place second cake, flat side up, on top of frosting. Frost sides and top of cake with remaining frosting.

Refrigerate leftovers.

Yield: 12-16 servings

Old Fashioned Crumb Cake

2 cups GF all-purpose baking flour
1 ⅓ cups granulated sugar
⅔ cup (5 ⅓ tablespoons) butter, softened
1 teaspoon xanthan gum
½ teaspoon salt
1 teaspoon baking soda
1 teaspoon ground cinnamon
½ teaspoon ground cloves
1 egg, beaten
1 cup buttermilk
¾ cup semi-sweet chocolate chips
¾ cup chopped walnuts

Preheat oven to 350°. Grease a 13-in. x 9-in. x 2-in. baking pan.

In a medium bowl, combine flour, and next four ingredients until crumbly. Set aside 1 cup for topping. Add baking soda and next two ingredients to remaining crumb mixture. Add egg and buttermilk; mix well. Pour into prepared baking pan.

Sprinkle with reserved crumb mixture; top with chocolate chips and nuts.

Bake for 30-35 minutes or until toothpick inserted in center comes out clean. Cool on wire rack.

Yield: 12-16 servings

> "Where there is cake, there is hope. And there is always cake."
> —Dean Koontz

Chocolate Peanut Surprise Cupcakes

1 ¾ cups GF all-purpose baking flour
½ cup unsweetened baking cocoa
1 teaspoon baking soda
¾ teaspoon xanthan gum
½ teaspoon salt
¾ cup (1 ½ sticks) unsalted butter, softened
1 cup granulated sugar
2 eggs
1 teaspoon vanilla extract
1 cup milk

PEANUT BUTTER FILLING:
½ cup creamy peanut butter
3 tablespoons unsalted butter, softened
1 ½ cups powdered sugar
3-6 tablespoons milk

CHOCOLATE FROSTING:
1 ½ cups milk chocolate chips
¾ cup sour cream
½ cup unsalted peanuts, chopped (optional)
Any remaining filling

Preheat oven to 350°. Grease or paper-line two 12-cup muffin pans.

Chocolate cupcakes: In a medium size bowl, whisk together the flour and next four ingredients.

In a large mixing bowl, beat butter and sugar until smooth and creamy, about 2 mintues. Beat in eggs and vanilla until fluffy. Gradually add flour mixture alternately with milk, beginning and ending with the flour mixture.

Fill prepared muffin cups two-thirds full. Bake for 15-20 minutes or until wooden pick inserted in centers comes out clean. Cool completely on wire rack.

Filling: In a medium size bowl, beat peanut butter and butter until smooth. On low speed, gradually beat in sugar and 3 tablespoons of milk. Beat on high speed until light and fluffy. Add more milk as necessary.

When cupcakes are cooled, carefully scoop out a portion of the top of cupcake using a melon baller or small cookie scoop. Spoon a heaping teaspoon of filling into cupcake. Place scooped out portion of cake back on top of cupcake, press down on top of filling. Use any remaining filling for the frosting.

Frosting: In a glass mixing bowl, melt chocolate chips in microwave, stirring every 30 seconds until melted and smooth.

With mixer on medium speed, beat in sour cream until fluffy and good spreading consistency. Stir in any left over filling. Frost cupcakes. Place chopped peanuts in a small bowl. Dip tops of cupcakes in chopped peanuts, if desired. Store, tightly covered in refrigerator up to 3 days.

Yield: 24 cupcakes

Spiced Zucchini Cupcakes with Caramel Frosting

3 eggs
1 ⅓ cups granulated sugar
½ cup canola oil
½ cup orange juice
1 teaspoon almond extract
2 ½ cups GF all-purpose baking flour
2 teaspoon ground cinnamon
2 teaspoon baking powder
1 ¼ teaspoon xanthan gum
1 teaspoon baking soda
1 teaspoon salt
½ teaspoon ground cloves
1 ½ cups shredded zucchini

CARAMEL FROSTING:
1 cup packed brown sugar
½ cup butter
¼ cup whole milk
1 teaspoon vanilla extract
1 ½ cups to 2 cups powdered sugar

Preheat oven to 350°. Grease or paper-line one 12-cup muffin pan and one 6-cup muffin pan.

In a large mixing bowl, beat the eggs and next four ingredients.

In a medium bowl, whisk together the flour and next six ingredients; gradually add to egg mixture and mix well. Stir in zucchini.

Fill prepared muffin cups two-thirds full. Bake for 20-25 minutes or until a wooden pick inserted in the center comes out clean.

Cool for 10 minutes before removing to a wire rack to cool completely.

For frosting, combing the brown sugar, butter and milk in a heavy saucepan. Bring to a full boil over medium heat; cook and stir constantly for 2 minutes or until thickened. Remove pan from heat and stir in vanilla. Cool to lukewarm.

Pour butter and sugar mixture into a medium mixing bowl; gradually beat in powdered sugar until frosting reaches spreading consistency. Frost cupcakes.

Yield: 1 ½ to 2 dozen

Cream Filled Carrot Cake

3 eggs
1 cup canola oil
1 ¾ cups granulated sugar
2 cups GF all-purpose baking flour
2 teaspoons baking soda
2 teaspoons ground cinnamon
1 teaspoon salt
1 teaspoon xanthan gum
¾ teaspoon ground cloves
¾ teaspoon ground ginger
¼ teaspoon ground nutmeg
3 cups shredded carrots
½ cup chopped walnuts

FILLING:
1 package (8 ounces) cream cheese, softened
¼ cup granulated sugar
1 egg

FROSTING:
1 package (8 ounces) cream cheese, softened
½ cup (1 stick) butter, softened
2 teaspoons pure vanilla extract
2 ½ - 3 cups powdered sugar

Preheat oven to 350°. Coat 10-in. fluted tube (Bundt) pan with cooking spray oil.

In a large mixing bowl, beat the eggs and oil until well blended. Add sugar and beat well.

In a medium bowl, whisk together the flour and next seven ingredients. Gradually add to egg mixture, combine well. Batter will be thick.

Add carrots and nuts, mix well.

Pour 3 cups of batter into prepared baking pan.

In a small bowl, beat cream cheese until fluffy; add sugar and beat well. Add egg and beat until smooth and creamy.

Spoon over batter. Carefully spoon remaining batter over filling.

Bake for 55-60 minutes or until a toothpick inserted near the center comes out clean. Cool 10 minutes before removing from pan to a wire rack to cool completely.

For frosting, in a small bowl, beat the cream cheese and butter until smooth. Add vanilla and beat well. Gradually add sugar until desired spreading consistency and sweetness is achieved.

Frost cake and store in refrigerator.

Red Velvet Cupcakes

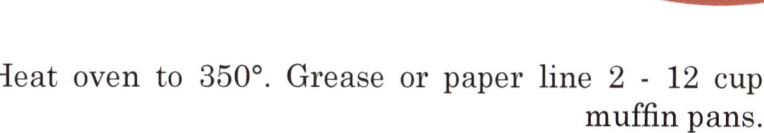

2 ½ cups GF all-purpose baking flour
1 ½ cups granulated sugar
1 tablespoon baking cocoa
1 teaspoon baking soda
1 teaspoon salt
1 teaspoon xanthan gum
¾ cup canola oil
¾ cup unsweetened applesauce
1 cup buttermilk, room temperature
2 large eggs, room temperature
1 tablespoon red food coloring
1 teaspoon white distilled vinegar
1 teaspoon vanilla extract

CREAM CHEESE FROSTING:
1 ½ sticks butter, softened
12 oz. cream cheese, softened
1 ½ teaspoons vanilla extract
3 ½ - 4 ½ cups powdered sugar

Heat oven to 350°. Grease or paper line 2 - 12 cup muffin pans.

In a medium bowl, whisk together the flour and next five ingredients.

In a large mixing bowl, mix together the oil and next six ingredients until well blended. Gradually add the dry ingredients to the wet ingredients and mix until smooth.

Fill prepared muffin pans 2/3 full with batter.

Bake for 20 – 22 minutes or until a toothpick inserted in the center comes out clean.

Remove from oven and cool completely on a wire rack.

Frost with your favorite cream cheese frosting.

FROSTING:

Cream together the butter and cream cheese until smooth; beat in vanilla. Gradually add powdered sugar until desired sweetness is achieved. Frost cupcakes.

Pineapple Cake with Coconut-Pecan Frosting

Preheat oven to 325°. Grease a 13-in. x 9-in. x 2-in. baking pan.

In a large bowl, combine butter, sugar and eggs; mix well. Stir in pineapple. In a separate bowl, whisk together the flour and next three ingredients. Stir into butter mixture along with the vanilla.

Pour batter into prepared pan. Bake for 40-50 minutes.

While cake is baking, prepare frosting as follows.

In a medium saucepan, combine butter, sugar and evaporated milk. Bring to a boil; boil for 4 minutes, stirring constantly. Remove from heat. Stir in coconut, pecans and vanilla.

Take cake out of oven and pour warm frosting over cake. Return cake to oven and bake for 10 more minutes or until icing is bubbly.

Yield: 18-24 servings

CAKE:
½ cup (1 stick) butter, melted
2 cups granulated sugar
2 large eggs, lightly beaten
1 (20-ounce) can crushed pineapple, undrained
2 cups GF all-purpose baking flour
1 tablespoon baking powder
1 teaspoon salt
1 teaspoon xanthan gum
1 teaspoon vanilla extract

FROSTING:
½ cup (1 stick) butter
1 cup granulated sugar
1 (5-ounce) can evaporated milk
1 ½ cups flaked coconut
1 cup chopped pecans
1 teaspoon vanilla extract

Cinnamon-Caramel Cupcakes

Heat oven to 350°. Grease or paper line 1 - 12 cup muffin pan and 1 – 6 cup muffin pan.

In a small bowl, whisk together the flour and next five ingredients.

In medium mixing bowl, beat butter and sugar for 1-2 minutes or until light and fluffy. Beat in eggs one at a time; add yogurt and mix well.

Beat flour mixture and caramel topping alternately into creamed mixture, ending with flour.

Fill prepared muffin cups two-thirds full.

Bake for 20-23 minutes or until toothpick inserted in center comes out clean.

Cool pans on wire rack for 5 minutes. Remove cupcakes to cooling rack to cool completely.

Prepare frosting while cupcakes are cooling. In a small, heavy duty saucepan, combine the chocolate and butter. Melt over low heat until chocolate is melted and mixture is smooth. Be very careful not to over cook this, chocolate will burn very easily.

Pour chocolate mixture into small mixing bowl; add caramel topping. Beat until well blended.

Gradually beat in 1-2 cups of powdered sugar, then gradually add milk, beating well after each addition. Gradually beat in remaining powdered sugar until mixture is smooth.

Let frosting stand at room temperature 15-30 minutes until a good spreading consistency is achieved. Liberally frost cupcakes.

Yield: 18

2 cups GF all-purpose baking flour
1 ½ teaspoons ground cinnamon
1 ½ teaspoons baking powder
1 teaspoon xanthan gum
½ teaspoon baking soda
¼ teaspoon salt
¾ cup (1 ½ sticks) butter, softened
$^2/_3$ cup granulated sugar
2 eggs
$^2/_3$ cup plain or vanilla yogurt
$^2/_3$ caramel ice cream topping

FROSTING:
6 ounces unsweetened baking chocolate
6 tablespoons butter
$^2/_3$ cup caramel ice cream topping
4 cups powdered sugar
$^1/_3$ cup milk

Mexican Cake

CAKE:
2 cups GF all-purpose baking flour
2 teaspoons baking soda
1 teaspoon xanthan gum
1 teaspoon ground cinnamon
2 cups granulated sugar
2 eggs, slightly beaten
1 can (20 oz.) crushed pineapple
1 cup coconut
1 chopped walnuts

FROSTING:
1 (8 ounce) package cream cheese, softened
½ cup (1 stick) butter, softened
2 teaspoons vanilla extract
3-4 cups powdered sugar

Preheat oven to 350°. Coat 9-in. x 13-in. baking pan with spray cooking oil.

CAKE:

In a medium bowl, whisk together the flour and next three ingredients.

In a large mixing bowl, beat together sugar and eggs; add pineapple and coconut, mix well. Stir in walnuts.

Pour batter into prepared baking dish and bake for 40-45 minutes or until a toothpick inserted in center comes out clean.

Cool completely on wire rack.

FROSTING:

In a medium mixing bowl, beat cream cheese until smooth. Add butter and beat together until smooth. Add vanilla, mix well. Beat in powdered sugar a little at a time until desired sweetness is achieved.

Frost cooled cake. Store leftover cake in refrigerator.

"A party without cake is really just a meeting."
-Julia Child

Apple Cake with Caramel Sauce

CAKE:
¼ cup (½ stick butter), softened
1 cup granulated sugar
1 egg
1 teaspoon vanilla extract
1 cup GF all-purpose baking flour
1 teaspoon baking soda
¾ teaspoon ground cinnamon
½ teaspoon xanthan gum
¼ teaspoon salt
¼ teaspoon ground nutmeg
2 medium tart apples, peeled and chopped

CARAMEL SAUCE:
½ cup (1 stick) butter
½ cup granulated sugar
½ cup packed brown sugar
¼ cup heavy whipping cream
¼ cup milk
Chopped walnuts, optional

Preheat oven to 350°. Grease an 8-in. square baking dish.

In a medium mixing bowl, cream together butter and sugar until smooth. Beat in egg and vanilla.

In a separate bowl, whisk together the flour and next five ingredients. Gradually add to butter mixture. Stir in apples and spoon batter into prepared baking dish.

Bake for 40-45 minutes or until a wooden pick inserted near the center comes out clean.

While cake is cooling, melt butter in a saucepan. Stir in the sugars, cream and milk. Bring to a boil over medium heat, stirring constantly. Reduce heat and simmer, uncovered for 15 minutes, stirring occasionally. Serve over warm cake.

Yield: 9 servings

Texas Sheet Cake

Preheat oven to 350°. Spray or grease 10-in. x 15-in. jelly roll pan.

In a heavy duty, small sauce pan over medium heat, combine butter and next two ingredients; bring to a boil.

Place chocolate mixture in mixing bowl and add sugar, eggs and sour cream; mix well.

In a medium bowl whisk together the flour and next three ingredients; gradually add to chocolate mixture. Beat until well combined.

Pour into prepared baking pan. Bake for 20-25 minutes or until toothpick inserted in center comes out clean.

Cool completely on wire rack.

ICING:

Once cake has cooled, in a heavy duty, small sauce pan over medium heat, bring butter, milk and cocoa to a boil.

Place chocolate mixture in mixing bowl and gradually add powdered sugar until desired consistency and taste is achieved. Beat well until all lumps are gone. Icing should resemble more of a glaze than traditional frosting.

Spread most of icing on cake, leave enough to coat marshmallows.

Coat marshmallows and spread evenly on cake. Sprinkle chopped nuts on top of marshmallows.

1 cup (2 sticks) butter
1 cup water
4 tablespoons baking cocoa
2 cups granulated sugar
2 eggs
1 cup sour cream
2 cups GF all-purpose baking flour
1 teaspoon baking soda
1 teaspoon xanthan gum
½ teaspoon salt

ICING:
½ cup (1 stick) butter
6 tablespoons milk
4 tablespoons cocoa
3-4 cups powdered sugar
2-3 cups miniature marshmallows, optional
2-3 tablespoons finely chopped walnuts, optional

Yields: 20-24 servings

"When someone asks if you'd like cake or pie, why not say you want cake AND pie?"
—Lisa Loeb

Pies & Cheesecakes

Oh how I looooooove a good cheesecake and might I add, I make a mighty tasty one—of course none of the ones you find here will be the run of the mill, plain cheesecake. Why make a plain one when you can have a turtle cheesecake or s'mores cheesecake, to name a couple? So many choices, so little time!

The pies I have added all use the same, really easy pie crust recipe. I used this pie crust as a demonstration speech when I was in Toastmasters. My mentor renamed it "The World's Best Pie Crust in the World!"—thus it's name. Not only is it super tasty (even those who do not have to be gluten free will LOVE this crust), but it is oh so easy! I never really did get the hang of rolling out pie crust dough. This crust is made entirely in the pie plate—super fast and easy!

Get ready to salivate all over these recipes…

World's Best Pie Crust in the World!
Blueberry Cheesecake Pie
Applesauce Walnut Pie
Brownie Bottom Cheesecake
Caramel Apple Pie with Pecans
Chocolate Chip Cookie Dough Cheesecake Pie
Mystery Pecan Pie
Rhubarb Strawberry Pie
Chocolate Chip Pie
S'mores Cheesecake
Strawberry Pie
Coconut Cream Pie
Turtle Pumpkin Cheesecake
Mock Apple Pie
Tin Roof Pie

World's Best Pie Crust in the World

1 ½ cups plus 3 tablespoons GF all-purpose baking flour
1 tablespoon granulated sugar
¾ teaspoon xanthan gum
½ teaspoon salt
½ cup vegetable oil
3 tablespoons milk

Preheat oven to 425° for baked pie crust.

Place flour and next three ingredients in pie pan.

Mix with your fingers until blended.

In a 1 cup liquid measuring cup, combine oil and milk; beat with a fork until creamy.

Pour milk mixture over flour mixture and mix with a fork until completely moistened.

Pat dough with fingers up the sides of pie pan first and then cover the bottom. Flute edges if desired.

Prick bottom of crust with fork and bake for 25 minutes. (You can also cover the crust with foil and place either pie weights on top of the foil or I use pinto beans.) Then bake as directed.

Blueberry Cheesecake Pie

1 World's Best Pie Crust, unbaked, using a 9-in. deep dish pie pan
2 packages (8 ounces, each) cream cheese, softened
½ cup granulated sugar
1 teaspoon vanilla extract
2 eggs, lightly beaten
2 cups fresh or frozen blueberries

Prepare pie crust.

Preheat oven to 350°

In a medium mixing bowl, beat the cream cheese, sugar and vanilla until smooth.

Add eggs; beat on low speed just until combined.

Fold in blueberries.

Spoon into prepared crust.

Bake for 35-40 minutes or until center is almost set. Check pie after 15-20 minutes to see if crust is browning too quickly. Cover with foil if necessary.

Cool on wire rack for 1 hour. Refrigerate until chilled.

Yield: 1 - 9" pie

Did you know?
Blueberries freeze in just four minutes.

Applesauce Walnut Pie

1 World's Best pie crust, unbaked
1 cup packed brown sugar
⅓ cup granulated sugar
1 tablespoon GF all-purpose baking flour
1 egg plus 1 egg white
½ cup unsweetened applesauce
2 tablespoons milk
1 teaspoon vanilla extract
1 cup chopped walnuts

Preheat oven to 375°.

Prepare pie crust.

In a large mixing bowl, combine sugars and flour. Beat in the egg, egg white and next three ingredients until well blended. Stir in walnuts.

Pour into prepared crust.

Bake for 40-45 minutes or until set. Cool completely.

Store in refrigerator.

Yield: 8 servings

> "Stress cannot exist in the presence of a pie."
> —David Mamet

Brownie Bottom Fudge Caramel Cheesecake

1 package GF fudge brownie mix (8-in. square pan size)
1 package (14 ounces) caramels
¼ cup evaporated milk
1 ¼ cups chopped pecans
2 packages (8 ounces each) cream cheese, softened
½ cup sugar
2 eggs
2 ounces semi-sweet baking chocolate, melted
2 ounces unsweetened baking chocolate, melted

Preheat oven to 350°. Grease a 9-in. springform pan.

Prepare brownie batter according to package directions. Spread into prepared pan. Bake for 15-20 minutes, do not over bake. Cool on wire rack while preparing caramel sauce.

In a microwave safe bowl, melt caramels with milk. Pour over brownie crust; sprinkle with pecans.

In a large mixing bowl, combine the cream cheese and sugar; beat until smooth. Add eggs, beating on low speed until just combined. Stir in melted chocolate, pour over pecans.

Bake for 35-40 minutes or until the center is almost set. Cool on wire rack for 10 minutes. Run a knife around the edge of pan to loosen; cool completely. Chill overnight. Remove sides of pan before serving.

Yield: 12 servings

Did you know?
Caramel was invented in 950 AD by Arabs.

Caramel Apple Pie with Pecans

1 World's Best Pie Crust, unbaked, using a 9-in. deep dish pie pan
7 cups peeled sliced tart apples
1 teaspoon lemon juice
1 teaspoon vanilla extract
¾ cup chopped pecans
⅓ cup packed brown sugar
3 tablespoons sugar
1 ½ tablespoons ground cinnamon
1 tablespoon GF cornstarch
¼ teaspoon nutmeg
¼ cup caramel ice cream topping, room temperature
3 tablespoons butter, melted

STREUSEL TOPPING:
¾ cup GF all-purpose flour
¼ cup granulated sugar
6 tablespoons cold butter, cubed
⅔ cup chopped pecans
¼ cup caramel ice cream topping, room temperature

Prepare pie crust.

Preheat oven to 350°

In a large bowl, toss apples with lemon juice and vanilla. In a medium bowl, combine the pecans and next five ingredients. Add to apple mixture and toss to coat apples.

Pour caramel topping over bottom of prepared pie crust; top with apple mixture (shell will be full). Drizzle with butter.

STREUSEL:

In a small bowl, combine the flour and sugar. Cut in butter until mixture resembles coarse crumbs. Stir in pecans; sprinkle over apple filling.

Bake for 55-65 minutes or until filling is bubbly and topping is browned. Immediately drizzle with caramel topping.

Cool on wire rack.

Yield: 8 servings

Chocolate Chip Cookie Dough Cheesecake

2 ¼ cup GF graham cracker crumbs
¼ cup granulated sugar
½ cup (1 stick) butter, melted

FILLING:
3 packages (8 ounces) cream cheese, softened
1 cup granulated sugar
3 eggs
1 cup sour cream
½ teaspoon vanilla extract

COOKIE DOUGH:
¼ cup butter, softened
¼ cup granulated sugar
¼ cup brown sugar, packed
1 tablespoon water
1 teaspoon vanilla extract
½ cup GF all-purpose baking flour
1 cup miniature semi-sweet chocolate chips

Place a greased 9-in. springform pan on a double thickness of heavy-duty foil (about 18 in. square). Securely wrap foil around pan.

Heat oven to 350°. Grease 9-in. springform pan.

In a small bowl, combine cracker crumbs and sugar; stir in butter. Press onto the bottom and up the sides of prepared pan; set aside.

In a medium mixing bowl, beat cream cheese and sugar until smooth. Add eggs; beat on low just until combined. Add sour cream and vanilla; beat just until blended. Pour over crust; set aside.

In a small mixing bowl, cream butter and sugars on medium speed for 3 minutes. Add water and vanilla. Gradually add flour. Stir in chocolate chips.

Drop dough by teaspoonfuls over filling, gently pushing dough below surface (dough should be completely covered by filling).

Bake for 45-55 minutes or until center is almost set.

Cool on a wire rack for 10 minutes. Carefully run a knife around edge of pan to loosen; cool 1 hour longer.

Refrigerate overnight; remove sides of pan.

Yield: 8-12 servings

Mystery Pecan Pie

1 World's Best Pie Crust, unbaked, using a 9-in. deep dish pie pan

CHEESECAKE LAYER:
1 package (8 ounces) cream cheese, softened
1/3 cup granulated sugar
1 teaspoon vanilla extract
1/8 teaspoon salt
1 egg
1 ¼ cup chopped pecans

PECAN LAYER:
2 eggs, slightly beaten
2/3 cup light corn syrup
¼ cup granulated sugar
1 teaspoon vanilla extract

Preheat oven to 375°.

Prepare pie crust.

In a medium mixing bowl, beat cream cheese and next three ingredients until smooth. Add egg; beat on low until just combined. Spread mix over bottom of unbaked crust.

Sprinkle pecans evenly over cream cheese mixture.

In medium mixing bowl, mix eggs and next three ingredients. Carefully pour egg mixture over pecan layer.

Bake for 40-45 minutes or until center is puffed and appears nearly set when gently shaken.

Cool on wire rack. Refrigerate before serving.

Yield: 8 servings

Did you know?
There are over 1,000 varieties of pecans.

Rhubarb-Strawberry Pie

TOPPING:
¾ cup GF all-purpose baking flour
½ cup brown sugar, packed
½ cup GF oats
½ cup (1 stick) cold butter, cubed

PIE CRUST:
1 World's Best Pie Crust

FILLING:
1 large egg
1 cup granulated sugar
2 tablespoons GF all-purpose baking flour
½ teaspoon ground cinnamon
1 teaspoon vanilla extract
1 – 1 ¼ lb. fresh rhubarb, cut in ½-in. pieces
2 cups fresh strawberries, cut in pieces
Zest from one medium orange

Did you know?
The leaves on the Rhubarb stalk are poisonous.

Preheat oven to 400°.

CRUST:

Place flour and next three ingredients in 9-in. deep dish pie pan.

Mix with your fingers until blended.

In a 1 cup liquid measuring cup, combine oil and milk; beat with a fork until creamy.

Pour milk mixture over flour mixture and mix with a fork until completely moistened.

Pat dough with fingers up the sides of pie pan first and then cover the bottom. Flute edges if desired.

FILLING:

In a large mixing bowl, beat the egg.

Beat in sugar and next three ingredients until well blended.

Add rhubarb, strawberries and orange zest, fold gently into egg mixture.

Pour into prepared pie crust.

TOPPING:

In a small bowl combine the flour, brown sugar and oats.

Cut in butter until mixture resembles coarse crumbs.

Sprinkle over fruit mixture.

Bake at 400° for 10 minutes. Reduce heat to 350° and bake for 45-60* minutes longer.

You may want to place foil or a drip pan under your pie plate as this is a full pie and the juice will bubble over.

*I bake with a stone pie dish and this pie baked for 1 hour and 35 minutes at 350°. I removed the pie from the oven when a knife inserted in the center did not meet any 'hard' pieces of fruit. I also watched for the sauce to start bubbling through the crumb topping.

Chocolate Chip Pie

1 World's Best Pie Crust, unbaked, using a 9-in. deep dish pie pan
2 large eggs
½ cup GF all-purpose baking flour
⅛ teaspoon xanthan gum
½ cup granulated sugar
½ cup packed brown sugar
¾ cup (1 ½ sticks) butter, softened
1 cup semi-sweet chocolate chips
1 cup chopped nuts, optional
Sweetened whipped cream or ice cream, optional

Preheat oven to 325°.

Prepare pie crust.

In a large mixing bowl, beat eggs on high speed until foamy.

In a medium bowl, whisk together flour and next three ingredients. Gradually add to eggs. Beat in butter. Stir in chocolate chips and nuts.

Spoon into prepared pie crust and bake for 60-70 minutes or until knife inserted halfway between outside edge and center comes out clean.

Cool on wire rack. Serve warm with whipped cream or ice cream.

Yield: 8 servings

"Chocolate is happiness that you can eat."
—Ursula Kohaupt

S'mores Cheesecake

Place a greased 9-in. springform pan on a single thickness of heavy-duty foil (about 18 in. square). Securely wrap foil around pan.

Heat oven to 325°. Grease 9-in. springform pan.

In a small bowl, combine cracker crumbs and sugar; stir in butter. Press onto the bottom and up the sides of prepared pan; set aside.

In a large mixing bowl, beat cream cheese, milk and vanilla until smooth. Add eggs; beat on low just until combined – do not over mix! Stir in chocolate chips and marshmallows. Pour over crust.

Place springform pan in a large baking pan; add 1 in. of hot water to larger pan.

Bake for 50-60 minutes or until center is almost set. Sprinkle with marshmallows. Bake for 4-6 minutes longer or until marshmallows are puffed.

Meanwhile, melt chocolate chips and shortening; stir until smooth. Drizzle over marshmallows.

Cool on wire rack for 10 minutes.

Carefully run knife around edge of pan to loosen; cool 1 hour longer. Refrigerate overnight. Remove sides of pan.

Yield: 12 servings

2 ¼ cups GF graham cracker crumbs
¼ cup granulated sugar
½ cup (1 stick) butter, melted

FILLING:
2 packages (8 ounces each) cream cheese, softened
1 can (14 ounces) sweetened condensed milk
2 teaspoons vanilla extract
3 eggs
1 cup miniature marshmallows
1 cup miniature semisweet chocolate chips

TOPPPING:
1 cup miniature marshmallows
½ semi-sweet chocolate chips
1 tablespoon shortening

Strawberry Pie

FILLING:

Wash, stem and cut strawberries into bite size pieces.

In a small saucepan, combine sugar, cornstarch and water. Boil until thick and clear. Add strawberry jello, stir until jello is dissolved.

Place cut up strawberries into prepared pie crust and pour thickened jello mixture over strawberries.

Chill until firm. Serve with whipped cream if desired.

Yield: 8 servings

1 World's Best Pie Crust, baked

FILLING:
1 quart fresh strawberries
¾ cup sugar
2 tablespoons cornstarch
1 ½ cups water
1 box (3 ounces) strawberry jello
Whipped cream, optional

Did you know?
Strawberries are the first fruit to ripen in the spring.

Coconut Cream Pie

1 World's Best Pie Crust, baked

PIE:
½ cup granulated sugar
3 tablespoons corn starch
1 tablespoon GF all-purpose baking flour
½ teaspoon salt
2 ¼ cups milk
3 large egg yolks (do NOT throw away the whites – will be used in meringue)
1 tablespoon butter
½ cup flaked coconut
1 teaspoon coconut extract

MERINGUE:
3 large egg whites
1 cup marshmallow cream
¼ cup flaked coconut
¼ teaspoon cream of tartar

Preheat oven to 350°.

In a heavy saucepan, mix sugar, cornstarch, flour and salt. Gradually whisk in milk. Bring to a boil; cook and stir 2 minutes or until thickened. Remove from heat.

In a small bowl, whisk a small amount of hot sugar mixture into egg yolks; return all to cooking pan, whisking constantly. Bring to a gentle boil. Cook and stir 2 minutes. Remove from heat; stir in butter, coconut and coconut extract.

Pour filling into prepared crust.

For meringue, in a mixing bowl, beat egg whites until soft peaks form. Gradually add marshmallow cream, beating on high speed. Continue beating until stiff glossy peaks form.

Gently spoon meringue over filling, covering entire pie. Sprinkle with remaining coconut and bake 12-15 minutes or until meringue is golden brown.

Cool 1 hour on wire rack.

Refrigerate at least 3 hours before serving.

Yield: 8 servings

Did you know?
Coconut is a drupe fruit (like a peach or plum), not a nut.

Turtle Pumpkin Cheesecake

FILLING:

¼ cup GF all-purpose baking flour
2 teaspoons ground cinnamon
½ teaspoon ground ginger
¼ teaspoon ground cloves
¼ teaspoon ground allspice
¼ teaspoon groung nutmeg
1 can (15 ounces) pumpkin (not pumpkin pie mix)
4 packages (8 ounces each) cream cheese, softened*
1 cup packed brown sugar
⅔ cup granulated sugar
5 eggs

CRUST:
1 cup GF all-purpose baking flour
⅓ cup packed brown sugar
¼ cup finely chopped pecans
½ teaspoon xanthan gum
6 tablespoons cold butter

TOPPING:
½ cup chopped pecans, toasted**
⅓ cup semi-sweet chocolate chips
1 teaspoon canola oil
½ cup caramel topping

Did you know?

Cheesecakes were served to athletes during the first Olympic games in 776 B.C.

Using bottom of 9-in. springform pan, cut a piece of parchment paper large enough to be placed inside bottom of pan. Spray bottom and sides of pan with cooking spray. Place parchment paper on bottom of pan, spray paper with cooking spray as well. Wrap pan securely with a double thickness of heavy-duty foil (about 18 in. square).

Heat oven to 325°.

In a small bowl, combine the flour, brown sugar, pecans and xanthan gum; cut in butter until crumbly. Press onto the bottom of prepared pan. Bake for 12-15 minutes or until set. Cool on wire rack for 5 minutes. Refrigerate about 5 minutes or until completely cooled.

In a small bowl, combine flour and next six ingredients; set aside.

In a large mixing bowl, beat cream cheese until smooth and creamy. Gradually beat in brown sugar and granulated sugar until smooth. On low speed, beat in eggs, one at a time, just until blended. Gradually beat in pumpkin mixture until smooth. Pour filling over crust.

Place springform pan in a large baking pan; add 1 in. of hot water to larger pan.

Bake for 1 ¼ to 1 ½ hours or until center is just set and top appears dull. Turn oven off; open oven door at least 4 inches. Let cheesecake remain in oven 30 minutes. Remove springform pan from water bath. Cool on wire rack for 10 minutes. Carefully run a knife around edge of pan to loosen; cool 1 hour longer. Refrigerate overnight.

Yield: 12-16 servings

*Recipe was tested with 2 packages of light cream cheese and 2 packages regular cream cheese.
**To toast pecans, sprinkle in ungreased heavy skillet. Cook over medium heat 5 to7 minutes, stirring frequently until pecans begin to brown, then stirring constantly until light brown.

Mock Apple Pie

1 World's Best pie crust, unbaked, using a 9-in. deep dish pie pan
6 cups peeled and seeded sliced zucchini, slice to resemble apple slices
1 ¼ cups granulated sugar
2 tablespoons GF all-purpose baking flour
2 ½ teaspoons ground cinnamon
1 ½ teaspoons cream of tartar
¼ teaspoon ground nutmeg
1 tablespoon butter, melted
1 tablespoon lemon juice

CRUMB TOPPING:
½ cup GF all-purpose baking flour
½ cup packed brown sugar
½ cup GF oats
⅓ cup chopped pecans, optional
4 tablespoons cold butter

Preheat oven to 375°.

Place sliced zucchini in large mixing bowl.

In a small bowl, combine sugar and next six ingredients. Stir into zucchini and let sit while preparing pie crust.

Pour zucchini mixture into prepared pie crust.

For topping, in a medium bowl, combine the flour and next three ingredients; cut in butter until mixture resembles coarse crumbs. Sprinkle over zucchini.

Bake pie for 50-60 minutes or until set. Check crust after 20-30 minutes to make sure it is not browning too much. Lightly cover with foil if necessary.

Yield: 8 servings

Did you know?
Settlers of the American west created this pie because they had no apples..

Tin Roof Fudge Pie

1 World's Best Pie Crust, baked, using a 9-in. deep dish pie pan
2 ounces semi-sweet baking chocolate
1 tablespoon butter

PEANUT LAYER:
1 package (11-14 ounces) caramels
⅓ cup heavy cream
1 ½ cups chopped, salted peanuts

CHOCOLATE LAYER:
8 ounces semi-sweet baking chocolate
2 tablespoons butter
1 cup heavy cream
2 teaspoons vanilla extract
Whipping cream and salted peanuts, optional

TOPPING:
3 caramels
5 teaspoons heavy cream
1 tablespoon butter

For crust, melt chocolate and butter in a double boiler. Stir until smooth. Spread chocolate mixture onto the bottom and up the sides of crust; refrigerate until chocolate is set.

Peanut layer: In a saucepan over low heat, melt caramels and cream, stirring frequently until smooth. Remove from the heat and stir in peanuts. Spoon into pie shell; refrigerate.

Chocolate layer: In a small saucepan over low heat, melt chocolate and butter. Remove from heat; let sit for 15 minutes.

Meanwhile, in a mixing bowl, beat cream and vanilla until soft peak forms. Carefully fold a third of the whipped cream into the chocolate mixture; fold in the remaining whipped cream. Spread over peanut layer; refrigerate until set.

Garnish with whipped cream and peanuts if desired.

In a small saucepan over low heat, melt caramels, cream and butter. Drizzle over pie. Refrigerate until serving.

> "Baking cookies is comforting."
> —Sandra Lee

Cookies

Cookies, probably my most favorite snack. If my freezer happens to be void of cookies, it is a sad day. This book contains many 'classic' cookies—oatmeal, snickerdoodles, peanut butter—yet most have a new twist to them. I have also included many 'fancier' types of treats that have become fan favorites. The S'mores Sandwich Cookie comes to mind! For these, I make the cookies and freeze them, then as I am ready to serve them I add the marshmallow and microwave it to become a s'more cookie. These also work great as your 'graham cracker' for actual s'mores to make over the campfire. My friends who do not need to be gluten-free love this version of the classic s'more!

A side story to the Vintage Sugar Cookie—the original of this recipe has been handed down in my family for at least 4 generations and we do not know how much earlier it has been around. It took me three years to gain the courage to convert this to gluten-free because I did not want it to taste any different. The few changes I made to the recipe were just perfect! I am totally amazed that they still taste just like they did to me as a child. I've had people tell me these are the most perfect cookie!

Ooey, gooey, crispy, chewy... These cookies have it all!

Vintage Sugar Cookies
S'mores Sandwich Cookies
Classic Oatmeal Raisin
Reverse S'oreos
Triple Chip Peanut Butter Cookies
Frosted Pumpkin Cookies
Chocolate Filled Snowballs
Cranberry Chip Cookies
Snickerdoodles
Double Chocolate Dream Cookies
Cherry Chocolate Shortbread
Spritz
Gingerbread Cut-Out Cookies
Chocolate Raspberry Cookies
Breakfast Cookies
Peanut Butter Sandwich Cookies
Classic Chocolate Chip Cookies

"C is for cookie. That's good enough for me."
-Cookie Monster

Vintage Sugar Cookies

½ cup shortening*
1 ½ cups granulated sugar
¼ cup milk
2 eggs
1 teaspoon vanilla extract
3 cups GF all-purpose baking flour, plus additional flour for rolling dough
2 ½ teaspoons baking powder
½ teaspoon salt
½ teaspoon xanthan gum
½ teaspoon ground nutmeg
¼ teaspoon ground cinnamon
Decorator sugars

FROSTING:
5 ⅓ tablespoons butter, softened
3-4 cups powdered sugar
¼ cup milk
1 ½ teaspoons vanilla extract

In a large mixing bowl, cream together shortening and sugar. In small bowl, lightly beat eggs and milk. Add vanilla and slowly add to creamed mixture.

In a separate bowl, whisk together the flour and next five ingredients. Gradually add to creamed mixture. Refrigerate dough for 1 hour or until easy to handle.

Preheat oven to 375° and line baking sheets with parchment paper.

On a lightly floured surface, roll dough out ¼ inch thick and cut with favorite cookie cutters. Sprinkle with decorative sugars.

Carefully place cookies on prepared baking sheets and bake for 8-10 minutes or until lightly browned.

Cool completely before frosting.

FROSTING:

In a small mixing bowl beat butter until fluffy. Gradually add one cup powdered sugar. Beat in milk and vanilla. Gradually beat in remaining powdered sugar until desired spreading consistency is achieved.

Yield: 3-4 dozen cookies

*recipe tested using organic shortening

S'mores Sandwich Cookies

¾ cup (1 ½ stick) butter
½ cup granulated sugar
½ cup packed brown sugar
1 egg
2 tablespoons milk
1 teaspoon vanilla extract
1 ¾ cups GF all-purpose baking flour
1 ¼ cups crushed GF graham crackers
½ teaspoon xanthan gum
½ teaspoon baking soda
¼ teaspoon salt
¼ teaspoon ground cinnamon
2 cups semi-sweet chocolate chips
24-28 Large marshmallows

Preheat oven to 375°. Line baking sheets with parchment paper.

In a large mixing bowl, cream butter and sugars. Beat in egg, milk and vanilla.

In a medium bowl, whisk together the flour and next five ingredients; gradually add to creamed mixture. Stir in chocolate chips.

Drop by tablespoonfuls 2 inches apart onto prepared baking sheets. Bake for 9-12 minutes or until golden brown.

Remove to wire racks to cool.

Place four cookies bottom side up on a microwave safe plate; top each with a marshmallow. Microwave on high for 15-20 seconds or until marshmallows begin to puff – do not over cook! Top each with another cookie. Repeat.

Yield: about 2 dozen sandwich cookies

Did you know?
The world's largest s'more ever made weighed 267 lbs.

Classic Oatmeal Raisin Cookies

1 ¼ cups (2 ½ sticks) butter, softened
¾ cup firmly packed brown sugar
½ cup granulated sugar
1 egg
1 teaspoon vanilla extract
1 ¾ cup GF all-purpose baking flour, sifted
1 ½ teaspoon ground cinnamon, heaping
1 teaspoon baking soda
½ teaspoon salt
3/8 teaspoon xanthan gum
¼ teaspoon ground nutmeg
3 cups GF oats
1 cup raisins

Preheat oven to 350°. Line baking sheets with parchment paper.

In a large mixing bowl, cream together butter and sugars on high speed. Add egg and vanilla; beat well.

In a separate large bowl, whisk together flour and next five ingredients.

Gradually add flour mixture to butter mixture. Add oats and raisins; mix well with mixer.

Scoop onto baking sheets using medium cookie scoop. Bake 6 minutes then turn baking sheets. Bake for an additional 2-3 minutes or until lightly browned.

Bake 6 minutes or until lightly browned.

Cool 1 minute on baking sheet; remove to a wire rack to cool completely.

Yield: 3-4 dozen

Did you know?

Oatmeal cookies are the #1 non-cereal usage for oatmeal.

Reverse S'oreos

Preheat oven to 350°. Line baking sheets with parchment paper.

In a small bowl, combine the vanilla, baking powder and salt. Stir to dissolve the baking powder; the salt will not completely dissolve.

In a large mixing bowl, beat together the sugar and butter; add the vanilla mixture. Beat until smooth.

In a medium bowl, whisk together the flour and xanthan gum. Gradually add to the sugar and butter mixture. Dough will seem dry at first, keep mixing until the dough comes together.

Using a small cookie scoop or teaspoon, scoop dough into 1" balls and place on prepared baking sheets.

Use the bottom of a glass*, dipped in sugar to prevent sticking, to flatten the balls to about ¼" thick.

Bake the cookies for 11-12 minutes or until they are lightly brown around the edges.

Cool on wire racks while preparing filling.

Place the chocolate chips, corn syrup and cream in a heavy saucepan. Heat mixture until the cream begins to form bubbles. Remove from heat, add vanilla and stir until smooth. Beat in powdered sugar.

Spoon a liberal amount of filling onto flat side of half of the cooled cookies. Top with another cookie and gently squeeze to push the filling out to the edges.

Store cookies in plastic wrap at room temperature.

Yield: 2 dozen sandwich cookies

*Instead of using a glass, if you have a food processor, the food pusher may have a circular, ridged pattern on the end of it which makes a nice design in the cookie.

COOKIES:
3 teaspoons vanilla extract
1 ½ teaspoons baking powder
1 teaspoon salt
1 ¼ cups granulated sugar
1 cup (2 sticks) unsalted butter, no substitutes
2 cups GF all-purpose baking flour
½ teaspoon xanthan gum

FILLING:
2 cups semi-sweet chocolate chips
1 ½ tablespoons light corn syrup
¾ cup heavy whipping cream
1 teaspoon vanilla extract
1 ½ cups powdered sugar

Triple Chip Peanut Butter Cookies

1 cup (2 sticks) butter, softened
1 cup creamy peanut butter*
1 cup granulated sugar
1 cup packed brown sugar
2 eggs
1 teaspoon vanilla extract
3 cups GF all-purpose flour
1 ½ teaspoons baking soda
1 teaspoon salt
¾ teaspoon xanthan gum
½ cup milk chocolate chips
½ cup semi-sweet chocolate chips
½ cup 60% bittersweet chocolate chips

Preheat oven to 325°. Line baking sheets with parchment paper.

In a large mixing bowl, cream the butter and next three ingredients. Add eggs one at a time and mix well. Add vanilla and mix well.

In a separate bowl, whisk together the flour and next three ingredients. Gradually add to creamed mixture and mix well. Stir in chips.

Scoop onto baking sheets using a medium cookie scoop or tablespoon. Bake 10-12 minutes or until lightly browned.

Remove from oven and cool for 5 minutes before removing from baking sheets to wire rack to cool completely.

Yield: 4 dozen

*Recipe was tested using Smart Balance™ Creamy Peanut Butter

Did you know?

The Aztecs invented peanut butter in the 14th century.

Frosted Pumpkin Cookies

1 cup (2 sticks) butter, softened
½ cup granulated sugar
½ cup packed brown sugar
1 egg
1 cup canned pumpkin
2 teaspoons vanilla extract
2 cups GF all-purpose baking flour
1 teaspoon baking powder
1 teaspoon baking soda
1 teaspoon ground cinnamon, heaping
½ teaspoon ground nutmeg
½ teaspoon xanthan gum
½ teaspoon salt
¾ cup chopped pecans, optional

CARAMEL FROSTING:
6 tablespoons brown sugar
4 tablespoons butter, no substitutes
6 tablespoons milk
3 ½ - 4 cups powdered sugar

Preheat oven to 350°. Line baking sheets with parchment paper.

In a large mixing bowl, cream butter and sugars. Beat in egg. Add pumpkin and vanilla.

In a medium bowl, whisk together the flour and next six ingredients. Gradually add to creamed mixture. Stir in pecans.

Drop by tablespoonfuls onto prepared baking sheets. Bake for 11-13 minutes or until edges are lightly browned.

Remove to wire racks to cool.

For frosting, in a small saucepan, bring brown sugar and butter to a boil. Cook and stir over medium-low heat for 1 minute. Do not over cook. Remove from heat and cool for 10 minutes.

Transfer to a medium bowl; beat in milk. Beat in enough powdered sugar to achieve spreading consistency. Frost cookies.

Yield: 3 ½ dozen

Chocolate Filled Snowballs

1 cup (2 sticks) butter, no substitutes
½ cup granulated sugar
1 teaspoon vanilla extract
2 cups GF all-purpose baking flour
½ teaspoon xanthan gum
1 cup chopped nuts
40 Hershey's Kisses
Powdered sugar for rolling

Preheat oven to 375°. Line baking sheets with parchment paper.

In a large mixing bowl, cream together the butter and sugar. Add vanilla and mix well.

In a medium bowl, whisk together the flour and xanthan gum. Gradually add to the butter mixture. Mix in nuts. Dough will be stiff.

Roll into balls large enough to shape around an individual kiss. Place dough covered kiss on prepared baking sheet and bake for 11-13 minutes or until lightly browned.

Cool completely on wire rack.

Roll cookie in powdered sugar.

Yield: 3 - 3 ½ dozen

Did you know?
70 million Hershey's Kisses are produced every day.

Cranberry Chip Cookies

1 cup butter (2 sticks), softened
¾ cup granulated sugar
¾ cup packed brown sugar
2 eggs
1 teaspoon vanilla extract
2 ½ cups GF all-purpose baking flour
1 teaspoon baking soda
⁵/₈ teaspoon xanthan gum
½ teaspoon salt
1 cup semi-sweet chocolate chips
1 cup vanilla chips
1 cup dried cranberries
1 cup chopped pecans

Preheat oven to 375°. Line baking sheets with parchment paper.

In a large mixing bowl, cream butter and sugars until light and fluffy. Add eggs, one at a time, beating well after each addition. Beat in vanilla.

In another bowl, whisk together the flour and next three ingredients. Gradually add to creamed mixture and mix well. Stir in chips, cranberries and nuts.

Drop by tablespoonfuls 2 inches apart on prepared baking sheets. Bake for 9-11 minutes or until golden brown.

Cool for 2-3 minutes before removing to wire rack to cool completely.

Yield: 5-6 dozen

Did you know?

Wisconsin is the largest producer of cranberries—my home state!

Snickerdoodles

½ cup shortening
½ cup (1 stick) butter
1 ½ cups granulated sugar
2 eggs
2 ⅔ cups GF all-purpose flour
2 teaspoons cream of tartar
1 teaspoon baking soda
⅝ teaspoon xanthan gum
¼ teaspoon salt
3 tablespoons granulated sugar
3 teaspoons ground cinnamon

Preheat oven to 400°. Line baking sheets with parchment paper.

In a large mixing bowl, cream together shortening, butter and sugar. Add eggs one at a time, mixing well after each addition.

In a medium bowl, whisk together flour and next four ingredients. Gradually add to creamed mixture.

In a small bowl, combine the remaining sugar and cinnamon.

Roll dough into balls the size of walnuts and roll in cinnamon/sugar mixture.

Place on prepared baking sheets. Bake for 8-10 minutes or until edges begin to brown.

Remove to wire racks to cool completely.

Yield: 4-5 dozen

Did you know?
This cookie was probably named after an early 1900s folk hero.

Double Chocolate Dream Cookies

2 ½ cups GF all-purpose baking flour
½ cup baking cocoa
1 teaspoon baking soda
⅝ teaspoon xanthan gum
½ teaspoon salt
1 cup (2 sticks) butter, softened
1 cup packed brown sugar
¾ cup granulated sugar
1 teaspoon vanilla extract
2 eggs
2 cups semi-sweet chocolate chips

Heat oven to 375°. Line baking sheets with parchment paper.

In a medium bowl, whisk together the flour and next four ingredients.

In a large mixing bowl, cream butter and sugars until light and fluffy. Add vanilla. Add eggs, one at a time, beating well for about 2 minutes or until light and fluffy.

Gradually add flour mixture to creamed mixture. Stir in chocolate chips.

Drop by rounded tablespoons onto prepared baking sheets.

Bake for 8-10 minutes or until cookies are puffed. Cool for 2 minutes; remove to wire racks to cool completely.

Yield: 4 ½ dozen

"A balanced diet is a cookie in each hand."
—Barbara Johnson

Cherry Chocolate Shortbread Cookies

1 cup butter, softened (no substitutes)
½ cup granulated sugar
½ teaspoon almond extract
2 cups GF all-purpose baking flour
¼ cup GF corn starch
½ teaspoon xanthan gum
¼ teaspoon salt
½ cup finely chopped dried cherries
¼ cup finely chopped semi-sweet chocolate chips
Granulated sugar

CHOCOLATE DRIZZLE:
½ cup semi-sweet chocolate chips
2 teaspoons shortening

Preheat oven to 300°. Line cookie sheets with parchment paper.

In mixing bowl, cream butter and sugar until fluffy, about 2 minutes. Add almond extract.

In a medium bowl, whisk together the flour and next three ingredients; gradually add to the butter mixture. Add cherries and chocolate.

Form dough into 1-inch balls and place on prepared baking sheets.

Pour a few tablespoons of sugar into a bowl or small plate; dip bottom of drinking glass in sugar and gently press down on each cookie to flatten.

Bake for 20-25 minutes or until bottoms begin to brown.

Cool 5 minutes; remove to a wire rack to cool completely.

Place chocolate chips and shortening in a small resealable freezer bag. Microwave on high for 30 seconds, until chocolate is almost melted. Knead bag to mix chocolate and shortening.

Snip off corner and drizzle over cookies.

Yield: 3 ½ - 4 dozen

Did you know?
January 3rd is National Chocolate Covered Cherry Day.

Spritz

2 ½ cups GF all-purpose baking flour
⅝ teaspoon xanthan gum
½ teaspoon salt
½ teaspoon ground cinnamon
1 cup (2 sticks) butter, no substitutes
1 – 3 oz. cream cheese
1 cup granulated sugar
1 egg yolk
1 teaspoon vanilla
Decorative sugars

Preheat oven to 350°.

In medium bowl, whisk together flour and next three ingredients.

In large mixing bowl, cream butter and cream cheese until light and fluffy. Gradually add sugar until well blended.

Beat in egg and vanilla, mix well.

Gradually add dry ingredients, mix well.

Pack dough into cookie press. Press cookies onto baking sheets. Sprinkle with decorative sugars if desired.

Bake for 10-12 minutes or until bottom just begins to brown.

Cool for 2-3 minutes before removing to cool completely on wire racks.

Yield: 3-4 dozen

Did you know?
"Spritzen" means "to squirt" in German.

Gingerbread Cut-Out Cookies

1 cup butter (2 sticks), softened
1 cup packed brown sugar
2 eggs
3 cups GF all-purpose baking flour
2 packages (3 ½ ounces each) cook-and-serve butterscotch pudding mix
3 teaspoons ground ginger
1 teaspoon ground cinnamon
1 teaspoon baking powder
¾ teaspoon xanthan gum

Preheat oven to 350°. Line baking sheets with parchment paper.

In a large mixing bowl, cream the butter and brown sugar until light and fluffy. Beat in the eggs.

In another large bowl, whisk together the flour and remaining ingredients. Gradually add to creamed mixture and mix well.

Cover and refrigerate for 1 hour or until easy to handle.

On a lightly floured surface, roll out dough to 1/4 –in. thickness. Cut with lightly floured cookie cutters.

Place one inch apart on prepared baking sheets and bake for 8-10 minutes or until firm. Let cool for 2-3 minutes before removing to wire racks to cool completely.

Yield: 2-5 dozen

"You can't catch me, I'm the Gingerbread Man!"
-The Gingerbread Man

Chocolate Raspberry Cookies

1 cup (2 sticks) butter, softened
¾ cup granulated sugar
¾ cup packed brown sugar
2 eggs
¾ cup semi-sweet chocolate chips, melted and cooled
½ cup seedless raspberry jam
3 cups GF all-purpose baking flour
¼ cup baking cocoa
¾ teaspoon xanthan gum
¾ teaspoon baking soda
¾ teaspoon salt
1 ½ cups vanilla chips

Heat oven to 375°. Line baking sheets with parchment paper.

In a large mixing bowl, cream butter and sugars until light and fluffy. Add eggs, one at a time, beating well after each addition. Beat in melted chocolate and jam.

In a separate bowl, whisk together the flour and next four ingredients; gradually add to creamed mixture. Stir in vanilla chips.

Drop by teaspoonfuls 2 in. apart onto prepared baking sheets. Bake for 10-12 minutes or until edges begin to brown.

Remove to wire racks to cool.

Yield: 6 dozen

Did you know?
Raspberries don't ripen after picking.

Breakfast Cookies

½ cup (1 stick) butter, softened
1 cup peanut butter
1 ¼ cups packed brown sugar
2 teaspoons vanilla extract
2 eggs
⅓ cup milk
1 ½ cups GF all-purpose flour
⅓ cup non-fat dried milk
1 teaspoon cinnamon, heaping
1 teaspoon salt
½ teaspoon xanthan gum
1 cup GF oats
1 cup coconut
1 cup semi-sweet chocolate chips
¾ cup chopped peanuts
¾ cup dried cranberries

Other add ins: raisins, GF granola, walnuts, pecans – need a total of 4 ½ cups of add ins.

Heat oven to 375°. Line baking sheets with parchment paper.

In a large mixing bowl, beat butter and peanut butter until smooth. Add brown sugar and beat until fluffy; add vanilla and beat until well combined.

Add eggs, one at a time until well combined. Beat in milk. Make sure to scrape bottom and sides of the bowl once or twice.

In a medium bowl, whisk together the flour and next four ingredients; gradually add to creamed mixture.

Stir in oats and next 4 ingredients. Drop by tablespoonful on prepared baking sheets.

Bake for 10-12 minutes or until lightly browned. Cool 5 minutes before placing cookies on wire rack to cool completely.

Yield: 4-5 dozen

"A cookie a day keeps the sadness away."

–Anonymous

Peanut Butter Sandwich Cookies

½ cup (1 stick) butter, softened
½ cup creamy peanut butter*
½ cup granulated sugar
½ cup packed brown sugar
1 egg
½ teaspoon vanilla extract
1 ½ cup GF all-purpose flour
¾ teaspoon baking soda
½ teaspoon salt
³⁄₈ teaspoon xanthan gum

FILLING:
½ cup creamy peanut butter*
2 cups powdered sugar
1 teaspoon vanilla extract
4-5 tablespoons milk

Preheat oven to 350°. Line baking sheets with parchment paper.

In a large mixing bowl, cream the butter and next three ingredients. Beat in egg and vanilla.

In a separate bowl, whisk together the flour and next three ingredients. Gradually add to creamed mixture and mix well.

Drop by rounded teaspoonfuls onto baking sheets. Flatten with a fork, dipping fork in powdered sugar to prevent cookie from sticking to fork if necessary. Bake 10-12 minutes or until lightly browned.

Remove from oven and cool for 5 minutes before removing from baking sheets to wire rack to cool completely.

For filling, in a large bowl, beat the peanut butter, powdered sugar and vanilla. Beat in enough milk to achieve spreading consistency. Spread filling on bottom of one cookie and top with a second cookie.

Yield: 18-20 sandwich cookies

*Recipe was tested using Smart Balance™ Creamy Peanut Butter

Did you know?

Peanuts are not nuts. They are legumes, like beans, peas, and lentils.

Classic Chocolate Chip Cookies

2 ¾ cups GF all-purpose baking flour
1 teaspoon baking powder
1 teaspoon salt
⅝ teaspoon xanthan gum
½ teaspoon ground cinnamon
1 cup (2 sticks) butter, softened
¾ cup granulated sugar
¾ cup brown sugar, packed
2 eggs
1 tablespoon molasses
1 teaspoon vanilla extract
2 cups semi-sweet chocolate chips

Preheat oven to 350°. Line baking sheets with parchment paper.

In a medium bowl, whisk or sift together the flour and next four ingredients.

In a large mixing bowl, cream together the butter and sugars. Add eggs, one at a time, beating well after each addition. Beat in molasses and vanilla.

Gradually add flour mixture, mixing well. Stir in chocolate chips.

Using a cookie scoop (I use a #40), scoop dough onto prepared baking sheets.

Bake for 8-11 minutes or until golden brown.

Cool on wire racks.

Yield: 5-6 dozen

Did you know?
The world's biggest chocolate chip cookie weighed 40,000 lbs.

"Stressed is 'desserts' spelled backwards."
—Unknown

Other Desserts

This section is devoted to one of my favorite pastimes... desserts. I love desserts and prefer to eat them first! The recipes in this chapter are among my favorites (as well as favorites of my daughter and doctor).

Sometimes you just need an extra special dessert. In the following pages you will find several options to meet the requirements of any special occasion you may want to give that extra special touch. These tasty treats are usually not 'quick' to make treats, but they're oh-so worth it... so plan accordingly.

Enjoy these delicious extra desserts!

Applesauce Drop Donuts
Blueberry Torte
Butter Brickle Biscotti
Mini Peanut Butter Cup Cheesecakes
Caramel Apple Crisp
Pumpkin Whoopie Pies
Strawberry Oat-Fashioned Dessert
Brownie Whoops
Blackberry Cobbler
Pumpkin Roll
Blueberry Apple Crisp
Brownie Trifle
Perfect Hot Fudge Sauce

Applesauce Drop Donuts

In a large mixing bowl, cream butter and sugar until light and fluffy, about 2 minutes. Add the eggs, one at a time, beating well after each addition. Beat in applesauce and vanilla.

In a medium bowl, whisk together the flour and next five ingredients; gradually add to the creamed mixture alternately with the milk (the batter will be thick).

In an electric skillet or deep-fryer, heat oil to 375°.

Using a small cookie scoop or teaspoon, drop spoonfuls of batter a few at a time into hot oil. Fry until golden brown on all sides.

Drain on paper towels; roll in sugar while warm.

Lindy's note: I rolled the finished donuts in a mixture of cinnamon and sugar. Also note that the larger you make them, the longer they will have to cook therefore the darker they will become. Mine were not golden brown due to using a medium cookie scoop.

3 tablespoons butter, softened
¾ cup granulated sugar
3 eggs
1 cup unsweetened applesauce
1 teaspoon vanilla extract
4 ½ cups GF all-purpose baking flour
3 ½ teaspoons baking powder
2 teaspoons xanthan gum
1 teaspoon salt
1 teaspoon ground cinnamon
¼ teaspoon ground nutmeg
¼ cup milk
Oil for deep-frying
Additional sugar

Did you know?
Over 10 billion donuts are made in the US every year.

Blueberry Torte

CRUST:
1 ½ cups GF graham cracker crumbs
¼ cup granulated sugar
6 tablespoons butter, melted

FILLING:
2 (8-oz.) packages cream cheese*
1 cup granulated sugar
4 eggs

TOPPING:
¾ cup granulated sugar
1/3 cup GF all purpose baking flour
2 teaspoons lemon zest
1 tablespoon fresh lemon juice
5 cups fresh or frozen blueberries
Whipping cream, optional

Preheat oven to 350°. Coat 13-in. x 9-in. baking pan with cooking spray oil.

For crust: Combine graham cracker crumbs and sugar in baking pan. Drizzle melted butter over crumbs. Mix with fork until crumbs are all moistened. Press evenly over bottom of pan.

For filling: In a large mixing bowl, whip cream cheese until light and fluffy. Add sugar and mix well. Add eggs, one at a time, until just combined. Pour filling over crust.

Bake for 25-35 minutes or until firm and light brown around edges.

Cool on wire rack.

While cheese cake is cooling, place all the topping ingredients in a heavy saucepan and cook over medium heat until thick. Mash a few of the berries as they are cooking. When desired thickness is achieved (should look like 'canned' pie filling), pour over cheesecake.

Serve warm or chilled–with or without whipped cream!

*I used one package of light (33% less fat) and one package of regular cream cheese for this filling.

> "I'm not a vegetarian, I'm a dessertarian."
> —Bill Watterson

Butter Brickle Biscotti

½ cup (1 stick) butter, softened
½ cup granulated sugar
¼ cup packed brown sugar
3 eggs
2 teaspoons vanilla extract
3 cups GF all-purpose baking flour
2 teaspoons baking powder
¾ teaspoon xanthan gum
¼ teaspoon salt
1 package (8 ounces) milk chocolate English toffee bits

Line baking sheet with parchment paper.

In a large bowl, cream butter and sugars until light and fluffy. Add eggs, one at a time, beating well after each addition. Beat in vanilla.

In a medium bowl, whisk together the flour and next three ingredients; gradually add to creamed mixture and mix well. Stir in toffee bits.

Divide dough in half. On prepared baking sheet, shape each dough half into a 10-in. x 2-1/2-in. rectangle. Cover and refrigerate for 30 minutes.

Preheat oven to 350°. Line baking sheets with parchment paper.

Bake for 30-35 minutes or until golden brown. Cool for 10 minutes.

Carefully transfer to a cutting board; cut diagonally with a serrated knife into ½-in. slices.*

Place slices cut side down on prepared baking sheets. Bake for 12 minutes, turn each slice over and bake for another 8-10 minutes or until golden brown.

Store in airtight container.

Yield: about 2-½ dozen

*For easier, neater slices, rinse knife off after every 2-3 cuts. The toffee tends to stick to the knife which keeps the knife blade from cutting through cookie cleanly.

Did you know?

Biscotti was a convenient food for Ancient Roman travelers.

Mini Peanut Butter Cup Cheesecakes

Preheat the oven to 350°. Paper-line one 12-cup muffin pan.

In a small bowl, combine the graham cracker crumbs, sugar and butter. Combine until nice and crumbly.

Place about a heaping tablespoon of the graham cracker mixture in each prepared muffin cup and press into bottom of cup using a spoon.

Remove the wrappers from the peanut butter cups. Place one peanut butter cup in the center of the crust in each cup.

Beat the cream cheese until nice and fluffy.

Add in the sugar, flour and vanilla and continue beating until well combined. Add in the eggs one at time making sure they are well incorporated. Do not overbeat.

Spoon the cream cheese mixture over the Reese's, evenly dividing the mixture among the 12 cups. I use about 1/4 c of the mixture for each cup. Bake for about 20-25 minutes until the cheesecakes are set.

Cool cheesecakes on wire rack.

While cheesecakes are cooling, melt the peanut butter chips and 1 teaspoon of shortening in the microwave and then use a fork to swirl the melted chips over the top of the cheesecakes. Do the same with the chocolate chips.

Store the cheesecakes in the fridge if you don't eat them all in one sitting.

*Recipe was tested using one package light cream cheese and one package regular cream cheese.

¾ cup GF graham cracker crumbs
3 tablespoons granulated sugar
3 tablespoons butter, melted
12 miniature peanut butter cups
2 packages (8 ounces each) cream cheese*, softened
1 cup sugar
¼ cup GF all-purpose baking flour
2 teaspoons vanilla extract
2 eggs, room temperature
½ cup peanut butter chips
½ cup semi-sweet chocolate chips
2 teaspoons shortening, *divided*

Caramel Apple Crisp

1 package (9 ounces) caramels
2 cups GF oats
1 1/3 cups GF all-purpose baking flour
1 cup packed brown sugar
1 teaspoon ground cinnamon
½ teaspoon xanthan gum
2/3 cup cold butter
6 cups thinly sliced peeled tart apples
1 cup apple juice or cider, *divided*

Unwrap all caramels and set aside.

Preheat oven to 350°. Grease a 9-in. square baking pan.

In a large bowl, whisk together the oats and next four ingredients. Cut in butter until crumbly. Press half of the mixture into prepared baking pan.

Layer with half the apples and half the caramels. Sprinkle 1 cup of oat mixture. Layer remaining apples, caramels and oat mixture.

Pour ½ cup apple juice over top.

Bake for 30 minutes. Drizzle with remaining cider; bake 15-20 minutes longer or until apples are tender.

Yield: 9 servings

Did you know?
Apple Crisp was first mentioned in 1924.

Pumpkin Whoopie Pies

PIES:

Preheat oven to 350°. Line baking sheets with parchment paper.

In large mixing bowl, cream sugar and oil. Add pumpkin, eggs and vanilla. Mix well.

In a separate small bowl whisk together next eight ingredients. Mix into wet ingredients.

Using a medium cookie scoop (#40), drop by scoopfuls onto prepared baking sheet, spacing about 1 inch apart.

Bake 10-12 minutes.

Cool on wire rack.

FILLING:

In small mixing bowl, beat egg whites until stiff. Add vanilla, butter flavoring and powdered sugar.

In a separate bowl, cream shortening and cream cheese. Add to egg white mixture. Beat on high until fluffy.

Spread liberally on half of pumpkin cookies and top with remaining cookies.

Wrap in plastic wrap and store in refrigerator or freeze.

We like these better frozen – but they are still tasty at room temperature.

Yield: 2 dozen

PIES:
2 cups brown sugar
1 cup canola oil
1 can (15 oz.) pumpkin
2 eggs
1 teaspoon vanilla extract
2 ¾ cups GF all-purpose flour
1 teaspoon xanthan gum
1 teaspoon baking soda
1 teaspoon baking powder
1 teaspoon salt
1 ½ teaspoons ground cinnamon
1 ½ teaspoons ground ginger
1 ½ teaspoons ground cloves

FILLING:
3 egg whites
3 teaspoons vanilla extract
½ teaspoon butter flavoring
3 cups powdered sugar
1 ½ cups shortening
3 oz. cream cheese, softened

Strawberry Oat-Fashioned Dessert

1 pound sliced fresh strawberries
½ cup GF all-purpose baking flour
½ cup GF oats
⅓ cup packed brown sugar
⅛ teaspoon baking soda
Pinch of salt
⅓ cup (5 ⅓ tablespoons) cold butter
1 tablespoon granulated sugar
1 teaspoon ground cinnamon, *divided*

Preheat oven to 350°. Grease a 1 quart baking dish. If using unglazed stoneware, no need to grease.

In a medium bowl, whisk together flour and next four ingredients. Whisk in ½ teaspoon cinnamon.

Using a pastry cutter, cut in butter until mixture resembles coarse crumbs. Reserve ½ cup for topping. Pat remaining crumb mixture into prepared baking dish.

In a medium bowl, combine sugar and remaining cinnamon; stir in strawberries.

Spoon over prepared crust. Sprinkle with the reserved crumb mixture.

Bake for 35-40 minutes or until golden brown.

Yield: 4 servings

"There is no better way to bring people together than with desserts."
-Gail Simmons

Brownie Whoops

PIES:

Preheat oven to 375°. Line baking sheet with parchment paper.

Place all baking chocolate and butter in a microwave safe bowl; heat for 30 seconds and stir. Continue this until chocolate is melted, decreasing cooking time as chocolate is melting. (Chocolate can burn very easily – so be careful not to over cook!)

In a separate bowl, whisk together sugar, eggs and vanilla; stir into chocolate mixture until smooth.

In a medium bowl, whisk together the flour and next four ingredients. Gradually stir dry ingredients into wet ingredients until moistened; do not over mix.

Using a medium cookie scoop (#40), drop by scoopfuls onto prepared baking sheet, spacing about 1 inch apart. Batter will make 24 'cookies'.

Bake for 8-9 minutes or until brownies spring back when lightly touched and a toothpick inserted into center comes out with a few crumbs on it.

Cool for 5 minutes on wire rack before removing from baking sheet to wire rack to cool completely. While brownies are cooling, prepare filling.

FILLING:

In small mixing bowl, beat egg whites until stiff. Add vanilla, butter flavoring and powdered sugar.

In a separate bowl, cream shortening and cream cheese. Add to egg white mixture. Beat on high until fluffy.

Spread liberally on half of brownie cookies and top with remaining cookies.

Wrap in plastic wrap and store in freezer. We like these better frozen–but they are still tasty at room temperature.

Yield: 1 dozen

PIES:
2 ounces unsweetened baking chocolate
4 ounces semi-sweet baking chocolate
½ cup (1 stick) butter
1 cup granulated sugar
3 eggs
1 teaspoon vanilla extract
1 cup GF all-purpose baking flour
¼ cup baking cocoa
½ teaspoon baking powder
½ teaspoon xanthan gum
½ teaspoon salt

FILLING:
1 egg white
1 teaspoon vanilla extract
¼ teaspoon butter flavoring
1 cup powdered sugar
½ cup shortening
3 ounces cream cheese, softened

Blackberry Cobbler

½ cup granulated sugar
4 ½ teaspoons quick-cooking tapioca
¼ teaspoon ground allspice
¼ teaspoon ground cinnamon
5 cups fresh blackberries*
2 tablespoons fresh lemon juice

DOUGH:
1 cup GF all-purpose flour
1/3 cup plus 1 tablespoon granulated sugar, divided
½ teaspoon xanthan gum
¼ teaspoon baking soda
¼ teaspoon salt
1/3 cup milk
1/3 cup vanilla yogurt
3 tablespoons butter, melted

Preheat oven to 350°. Coat a 2-quart baking dish with cooking spray.

In a large bowl, combine the sugar and next three ingredients. Add blackberries and lemon juice; toss to coat.

Let stand 15 minutes. Prepare dough while berries are standing.

Spoon berries into prepared baking dish.

In a medium bowl, whisk together the flour, 1/3 cup sugar and next three ingredients.

In a 1 cup liquid measuring cup, whisk together the milk, yogurt and butter; stir into dry ingredients until smooth.

Spread over the berry mixture.

Bake for 20 minutes. Sprinkle with remaining sugar. Bake 25-30 minutes longer or until golden brown.

Serve warm.

Yield: 10 servings

*Frozen blackberries may be used, thaw first.

Did you know?
Blackberries are a superfood with over 15 vitamins and minerals.

Pumpkin Roll

Preheat oven to 350°. Coat a 17 ½ in. x 12 ½ in. jelly roll pan with cooking spray oil, or line pan with parchment paper

In a medium mixing bowl, beat the eggs, sugar, pumpkin and lemon juice for 5 minutes.

In another medium bowl, whisk together the flour and next six ingredients.

Gradually add the flour mixture to the egg mixture, beat until fully combined.

Spread batter in prepared baking pan. Sprinkle dough with pecans.

Bake for 10-14 minutes or until toothpick inserted in center comes out clean.

Let cake cool for 5 minutes.

Invert the cake onto a wire rack, peel off parchment paper. Sprinkle powdered sugar on large towel and carefully transfer the warm cake to the towel, folding the sides of the towel over the cake. (Make sure to use plenty of sugar on towel so cake will not stick to towel.)

Roll the cake up in the towel and cool in the refrigerator thoroughly for about 45 minutes.

In a small mixing bowl, beat cream cheese and butter together until smooth. Beat in vanilla. Gradually add the powdered sugar. Beat until smooth.

Carefully unroll cooled cake, spread cream cheese mixture evenly over cake. Re-roll the cake, wrap in plastic wrap and refrigerate until ready to serve.

Slice cake and dust with more powdered sugar.

This cake is best served 1 – 2 days after making it for the flavors to fully develop.

3 eggs
1 cup granulated sugar
²⁄₃ cup canned pumpkin
1 teaspoon lemon juice
¾ cup GF all-purpose baking flour
2 teaspoons ground cinnamon, heaping
1 teaspoon baking powder
½ teaspoon salt
½ teaspoon ground ginger
½ teaspoon ground cloves
¼ teaspoon xanthan gum
1 cup pecans, chopped fine

FILLING:
1 cup powdered sugar plus more for dusting tea or flour sack towel
1 – 8 ounce package cream cheese, softened
½ cup (1 stick) butter, softened
½ teaspoon vanilla extract

Blueberry Apple Crisp

3 medium tart apples
2 cups fresh or frozen blueberries*
1 tablespoon GF all-purpose baking flour
¼ cup granulated sugar
1 teaspoon ground cinnamon
⅓ cup GF oats
¼ cup GF all-purpose baking flour
¼ cup brown sugar, packed
⅓ cup pecans, chopped
2 tablespoons butter, melted

Preheat oven to 400°. Coat a 2-quart baking dish with cooking spray.

Peel, core and thinly slice apples.

In a large bowl, combine the flour, sugar and cinnamon; add apple slices and blueberries. Toss to coat. Pour fruit into prepared baking dish.

In a small bowl, mix oats and next four ingredients until mixture is crumbly.

Sprinkle topping evenly over fruit and bake 25-30 minutes or until topping is browned and apples are tender when pierced.

Serve warm or cool.

*If using frozen berries do not thaw first.

Yield: 4-6 servings

Did you know?

Blueberries are one of the only foods that are naturally blue in color.

Brownie Trifle

Plan ahead—needs to chill.

1 9-in. x 13-in. pan of GF brownies cut into 1-in. cubes
2 packages (3 oz.) cook and serve chocolate pudding mix
2 cups heavy whipping cream
¼ cup powdered sugar
1 teaspoon vanilla extract
½ cup toffee bits
Baking cocoa

Prepare pudding according to package directions and chill for one hour.

Place half of cubed brownies in bottom of trifle bowl or other appropriate serving dish. Layer with half of pudding.

In a small mixing bowl, whip the cream, powdered sugar and vanilla until stiff peaks form. Spread half of cream over pudding layer. Sprinkle with toffee bits.

Repeat layers of brownies, pudding, whipped cream and toffee. Dust with cocoa.

Chill until ready to serve.

Yield: 10-15 servings

"Don't wreck a sublime chocolate experience by feeling guilty."
-Lora Brody

Perfect Hot Fudge Sauce

1 can (14 ounces) sweetened condensed milk
4 ounces semi-sweet baking chocolate
2 tablespoons butter (no substitutes)
1 ½ teaspoons vanilla extract

In a heavy saucepan, combine the milk, chocolate and butter.

Cook and stir over medium-low heat until chocolate is melted.

Remove from heat; stir in vanilla.

Yield: about 1 ½ cups

> "Desserts are the most crucial part of any meal."
> –Linda Sunshine

Breakfast is probably my most favorite meal of the day—especially on the weekend when I allow myself to make up one of these yummy treats that are to follow!

One tip that I learned the hard way, is when you are using xanthan gum, it needs to be added to the dry ingredients. If you forget to add it and wait until you have already added the wet ingredients it will not work like it needs to—at least in my experience. I have had to throw out several pancake batters because I forgot to add the xanthan gum, then put it in after all the batter was mixed up. The batter never became thick like pancake/waffle batter should. So since this is the breakfast book and there are several pancake/waffle recipes in here—I thought it wise to help you learn from my mistake. Now if you are using a flour mixture that already has the xanthan gum included—you have no worries.

Happy Breakfast making!

Pumpkin Waffles
Banana Blueberry Pancakes
Berries 'n Cream French Toast
Blueberry Poppy Seed Brunch Cake
LaValliere Breakfast Puffs
Caramel French Toast
Crispy Granola Bars
Nutty French Toast
Bonnie's Granola

Pumpkin Waffles

2 cups GF all-purpose flour
2 tablespoons sugar
1 tablespoon plus 1 teaspoon baking powder
1 teaspoon xanthan gum
1 teaspoon salt
1 teaspoon cinnamon
½ teaspoon nutmeg
½ teaspoon cloves
4 large eggs, separated
1 ½ cups milk
1 cup canned pumpkin
½ cup butter, melted

In a large bowl, whisk together first eight ingredients. Make a well in center of mixture.

In a medium bowl, whisk together egg yolks and next three ingredients. Add to flour mixture, stirring just until dry ingredients are moistened – scrape sides and bottom of bowl to make sure all flour is moistened.

In a small mixing bowl, beat egg whites at high speed until stiff peaks form. Gently fold into pumpkin mixture.

Pour about ¼ cup batter for each waffle onto a hot, lightly greased waffle iron.

Cook waffles until they easily release from waffle iron.

Yield: about 8 waffles

Did you know?

The largest pumpkin ever grown weighed 1,140 pounds.

Banana Blueberry Pancakes

1 ½ cup GF all-purpose baking flour
2 tablespoons granulated sugar
2 teaspoons baking powder
1 teaspoon ground cinnamon
¾ teaspoon xanthan gum
½ teaspoon salt
1 egg, lightly beaten
1 ¼ cups milk*
2 medium, ripe bananas, mashed
1 teaspoon vanilla extract
1 ½ cups fresh or frozen blueberries

In a large bowl, whisk together the flour and next five ingredients.

In a medium bowl, combine the egg and next three ingredients; stir into dry ingredients until just moistened. Fold in blueberries.

Poor batter by ¼ cupfuls onto a hot griddle. Turn when bubbles begin to form on top and sides begin to look dry.

Cook until second side is golden brown.

Yield: 12-14 pancakes

Note: If using frozen berries, do not thaw.

*Recipe was tested using 2% milk

Did you know?

Pancakes are found in almost every culture.

Berries 'n Cream French Toast

2 packages (3 ounces each) cream cheese, softened
½ cup marshmallow crème
½ teaspoon vanilla extract
2 cups slices fresh or frozen strawberries
¼ cup granulated sugar
1 ½ teaspoons GF cornstarch
1 tablespoon cold water
3 eggs
¾ cup milk
1 teaspoon ground cinnamon
8 slices GF bread

In a small bowl, beat the cream cheese, marshmallow crème and vanilla until smooth; set aside.

For syrup, in a small saucepan, bring strawberries and sugar to a boil. Reduce heat; simmer, uncovered, for 10 minutes.

Combine the cornstarch and cold water until smooth; stir into berry mixture. Return to a boil; cook and stir for 2 minutes or until thickened. Remove from the heat; keep warm.

In a shallow bowl, whisk the eggs, milk and cinnamon; dip both sides of bread in egg mixture.

On a lightly greased hot griddle, cook bread over medium heat for 2 minutes on each side or until golden brown.

To serve, spread each piece of French toast with cream cheese mixture; top with strawberry syrup.

Yield: 4 servings

Did you know?

In medieval times French toast was only enjoyed by the wealthy.

Blueberry Poppy Seed Brunch Cake

½ cup (1 stick) butter, softened
⅔ cup granulated sugar
1 egg
1 ½ cups GF all-purpose baking flour
2 tablespoons poppy seeds
¾ teaspoon xanthan gum
½ teaspoon ground cinnamon
½ teaspoon baking powder
¼ teaspoon baking soda
¼ teaspoon salt
½ cup sour cream
1 tablespoon grated lemon peel

TOPPING:
⅓ cup granulated sugar
2 teaspoon GF all-purpose baking flour
½ teaspoon ground nutmeg
2 cups fresh or frozen unsweetened blueberries

GLAZE:
½ cup powdered sugar
1 ½ teaspoons lemon juice
1 ½ teaspoon milk

Preheat oven to 350°. Spray 9-in. springform pan with cooking oil.

In a medium mixing bowl, cream butter and sugar until light and fluffy, about 2 minutes. Beat in egg.

In a medium bowl, whisk together the flour and next six ingredients; add to the creamed mixture alternately with sour cream.

Beat until just combined. Stir in lemon peel. Spread into prepared pan.

For topping, in a small bowl, combine the sugar, flour and nutmeg; gently stir in blueberries until coated. Sprinkle over batter.

Bake for 45-50 minutes or until a toothpick inserted near the center comes out clean. Cool for 10 minutes on a wire rack; remove sides of pan.

For glaze, whisk powdered sugar, lemon juice and milk until smooth; drizzle over cake.

Refrigerate leftovers.

Yield: 8 servings

"LaValliere" Breakfast Puffs

⅓ cup shortening
½ cup granulated sugar
1 egg
1 ½ cups GF all-purpose baking flour
1 ½ teaspoons baking powder
¾ teaspoons xanthan gum
½ teaspoon salt
½ teaspoon ground cinnamon
¼ teaspoon ground nutmeg
½ cup milk

TOPPING:
6 tablespoons butter, melted
½ cup granulated sugar
1 teaspoon ground cinnamon

Preheat oven to 350°. Grease 24-cup mini muffin pan.

In large mixing bowl, cream together shortening and sugar; add egg, mix well.

In a medium bowl whisk together flour and next five ingredients.

Mix dry ingredients alternately with milk on low speed, beginning and ending with flour mixture.

Fill prepared muffin cups 2/3 full. Bake for 15-20 minutes or until golden brown.

While puffs are baking, melt butter. In a small bowl, mix together sugar and cinnamon.

Immediately roll in melted butter then roll in cinnamon and sugar mixture.

Serve warm.

Yield: 24 mini puffs

"One should not attend even the end of the world without a good breakfast."
-Robert A. Heinlein

Caramel French Toast

½ cup brown sugar, packed
¼ cup (½ stick) butter
1 tablespoon corn syrup
3 slices GF bread
3 eggs
¾ milk or half-and-half cream
½ teaspoon vanilla extract
½ teaspoon ground cinnamon
¼ teaspoon salt

Coat an 8-inch square baking dish with cooking spray.

In a heavy, small saucepan, bring the brown sugar, butter and corn syrup to a boil over medium heat, stirring constantly.

Remove from heat. Pour into prepared baking dish.

Arrange bread over caramel.

In a small bowl, whisk together the eggs and next three ingredients; pour over bread.

Cover and refrigerate overnight.

Remove from refrigerator 30 minutes before baking. Bake, uncovered at 350° for 25-30 minutes or until a knife inserted near the center comes out clean.

Yield: 2 servings

Did you know?
Milton Hershey began his chocolate empire with caramel.

Crispy Granola Bars

2 eggs
½ cup canola oil
½ cup packed brown sugar
3 cups GF oats
1 tablespoon baking powder
1 ½ teaspoons ground cinnamon
1 teaspoon salt
½ cup flaked coconut
½ cup raisins
½ cup chopped walnuts
½ cup semi-sweet chocolate chips

Heat oven to 350°. Grease 13" x 9" baking pan.

In a small bowl, combine eggs, oil and brown sugar.

In a medium bowl, combine oats and next three ingredients; add egg mixture to dry ingredients, stirring just until moistened. Stir in coconut and next three ingredients.

Spread into prepared pan. Bake, uncovered for 20-25 minutes or until edges are golden brown.

Cool for 5 minutes and cut into bars.

Did you know?
January 21st is National Granola Bar Day.

Nutty French Toast

4-5 slices GF bread—enough to cover bottom of 8-in. square baking pan
4 eggs
1 cup milk
1 teaspoon vanilla extract
½ teaspoon ground cinnamon
6 tablespoons (¾ stick) butter
⅔ cup packed brown sugar
1 ½ tablespoons dark corn syrup
½ cup chopped walnuts

Place bread in a greased 8-in. square baking dish.

In a large bowl, beat eggs and next three ingredients; pour over bread.

Cover and refrigerate overnight.

Remove from the refrigerator 30 minutes before baking.

Preheat oven to 350°.

While casserole is warming up, cream butter, brown sugar and syrup until smooth; carefully spread over bread. Sprinkle with nuts.

Bake, uncovered for 1 hour or until golden brown.

Yield: 4 servings

"Sometimes I've believed as many as six impossible things before breakfast."
-Lewis Carroll

Bonnie's Excellent Granola

3 cups gluten-free rolled oats
2 tablespoons packed brown sugar
½ cup chopped almonds
⅓ cup chopped walnuts
½ teaspoon ground cinnamon
⅓ teaspoon salt*
⅓ cup canola oil
⅓ cup honey

Preheat oven to 335°. Coat 10-in. x 15-in. baking sheet with cooking spray oil.

In a large bowl, combine oats and next five ingredients. In a liquid measuring cup, whisk together the oil and honey; pour over dry ingredients and mix thoroughly.

Spread in prepared baking pan. Bake for 15 minutes; remove from oven and stir. Return to oven for 10 minutes; remove from oven and stir again. Return to oven for 7 minutes; remove from oven and stir again. If granola still seems too moist, return to oven for 2-3 minutes; remove and stir again.

Granola should be golden brown in color when done.

Cool granola completely on wire rack, stirring several times to break up any large pieces.

Store in air tight container when completely cooled.

*Recipe was tested with both sea salt and Kosher salt.

Lindy's note: I bake this in a stone bar pan—when using stone, there is no need to coat the pan with cooking spray oil.

Check Out Lindy's Other Book!

Looking for **Gluten-free** recipes that require **no guesswork?**

Need a cake, cookies, muffins or pie that will **show you care** about your gluten-free family member, or friends?

Lindy's Gluten-Free Goodies and More is the recipe book for you!

Lindy has taken the guesswork out of what works and what doesn't with **101 recipes** that have **been tested** by those who suffer from being gluten intolerant and celiac disease as well as those who don't. From **cookies and cakes** to brownies and pies, you **won't have to worry**. This is your **one place** to go to **satisfy everyone's** sweet tooth.

Follow Lindy at Facebook.com/LindysGlutenFreeGoodies

Order this book on Amazon.com or at any bookstore!